SUPERMAN BATMAN
VENGEANCE

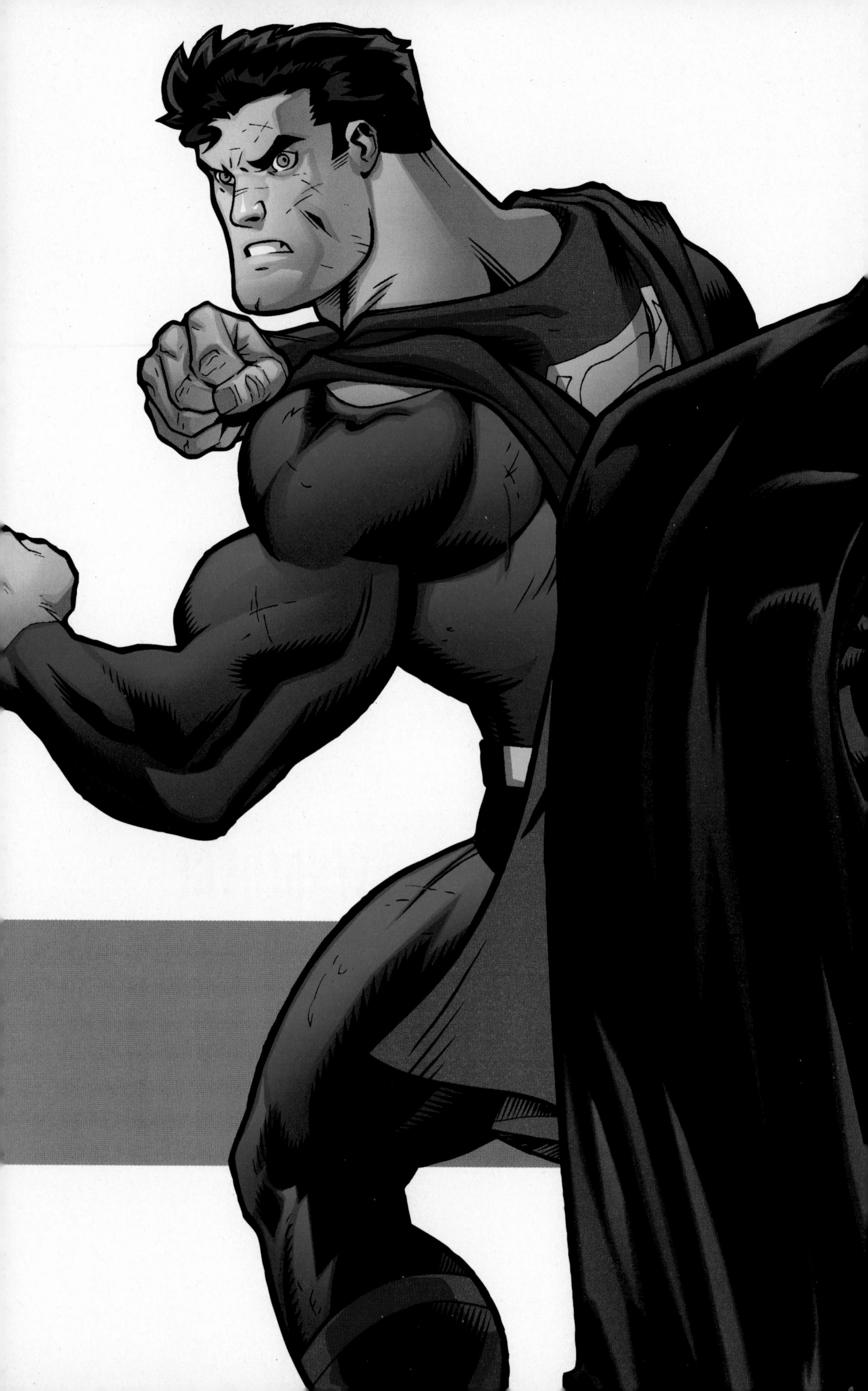

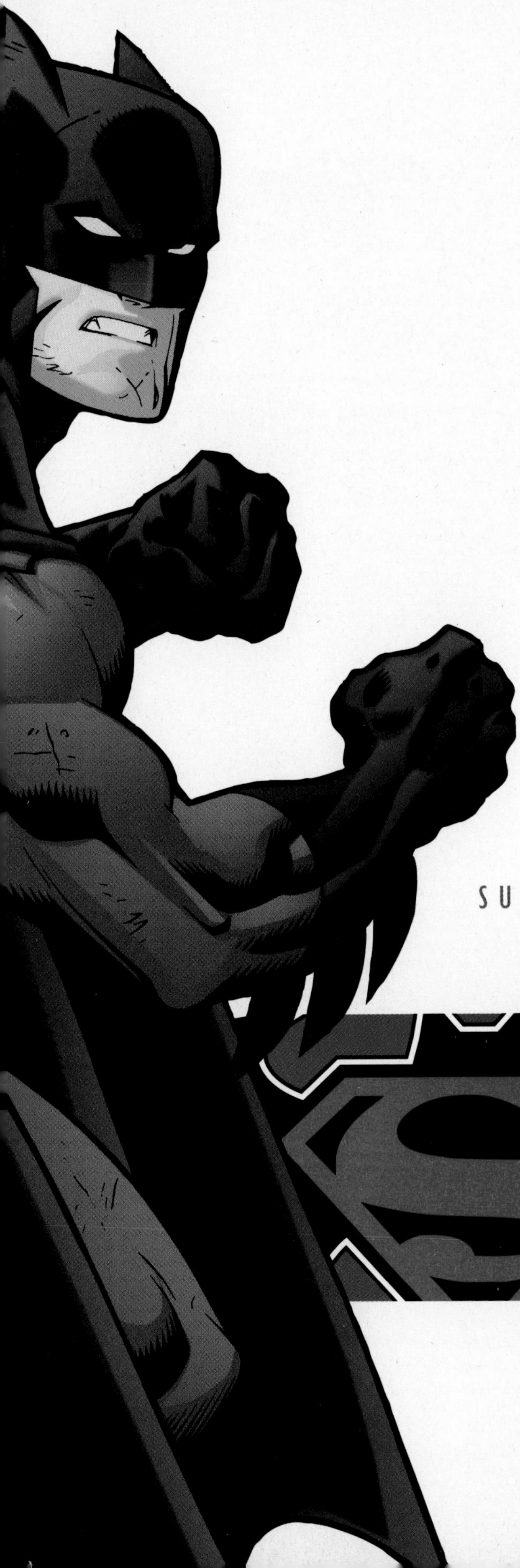

Jeph Loeb
Writer

Ed McGuinness
Penciller

Dexter Vines
Inker

Lee Loughridge
Dave McCaig
Colorists

Richard Starkings
Letterer

Ed McGuinness & Dexter Vines
Original series covers

Batman created by Bob Kane

Superman created by Jerry Siegel and Joe Shuster

SUPERMAN BATMAN
VENGEANCE

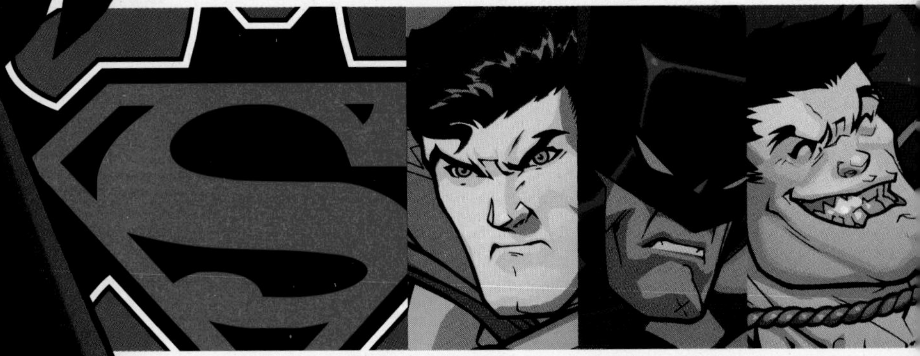

DAN DIDIO Senior VP-Executive Editor   EDDIE BERGANZA Editor-original series   TOM PALMER, JR. Associate Editor-original series   BOB JOY Editor-collected edition
ROBBIN BROSTERMAN Senior Art Director   PAUL LEVITZ President & Publisher   GEORG BREWER VP-Design & DC Direct Creative   RICHARD BRUNING Senior VP-Creative Director
PATRICK CALDON Executive VP-Finance & Operations   CHRIS CARAMALIS VP-Finance   JOHN CUNNINGHAM VP-Marketing   TERRI CUNNINGHAM VP-Managing Editor
STEPHANIE FIERMAN Senior VP-Sales & Marketing   ALISON GILL VP-Manufacturing   RICH JOHNSON VP-Book Trade Sales   HANK KANALZ VP-General Manager, WildStorm
LILLIAN LASERSON Senior VP & General Counsel   JIM LEE Editorial Director-WildStorm   PAULA LOWITT Senior VP-Business & Legal Affairs
DAVID MCKILLIPS VP-Advertising & Custom Publishing   JOHN NEE VP-Business Development   GREGORY NOVECK Senior VP-Creative Affairs
CHERYL RUBIN Senior VP-Brand Management   JEFF TROJAN VP-Business Development, DC Direct   BOB WAYNE VP-Sales

SUPERMAN/BATMAN: VENGEANCE
Published by DC Comics. Cover, sketch gallery and compilation copyright © 2006 DC Comics. All Rights Reserved.
Originally published in single magazine form in SUPERMAN/BATMAN #20-25. Copyright © 2005, 2006 DC Comics. All Rights Reserved. All characters, their distinctive
likenesses and related elements featured in this publication are trademarks of DC Comics. The stories, characters and incidents featured in this publication are entirely fictional.
DC Comics does not read or accept unsolicited submissions of ideas, stories or artwork.
DC Comics, 1700 Broadway, New York, NY 10019. A Warner Bros. Entertainment Company. Printed in Canada. First Printing.
Hardcover ISBN: 1-4012-0921-1.   Hardcover ISBN 13: 978-1-4012-0921-6.   Softcover ISBN: 1-4012-1043-0.   Softcover ISBN 13: 978-1-4012-1043-4.
Cover art by Ed McGuinness and Dexter Vines. All covers colored by Dave McCaig.

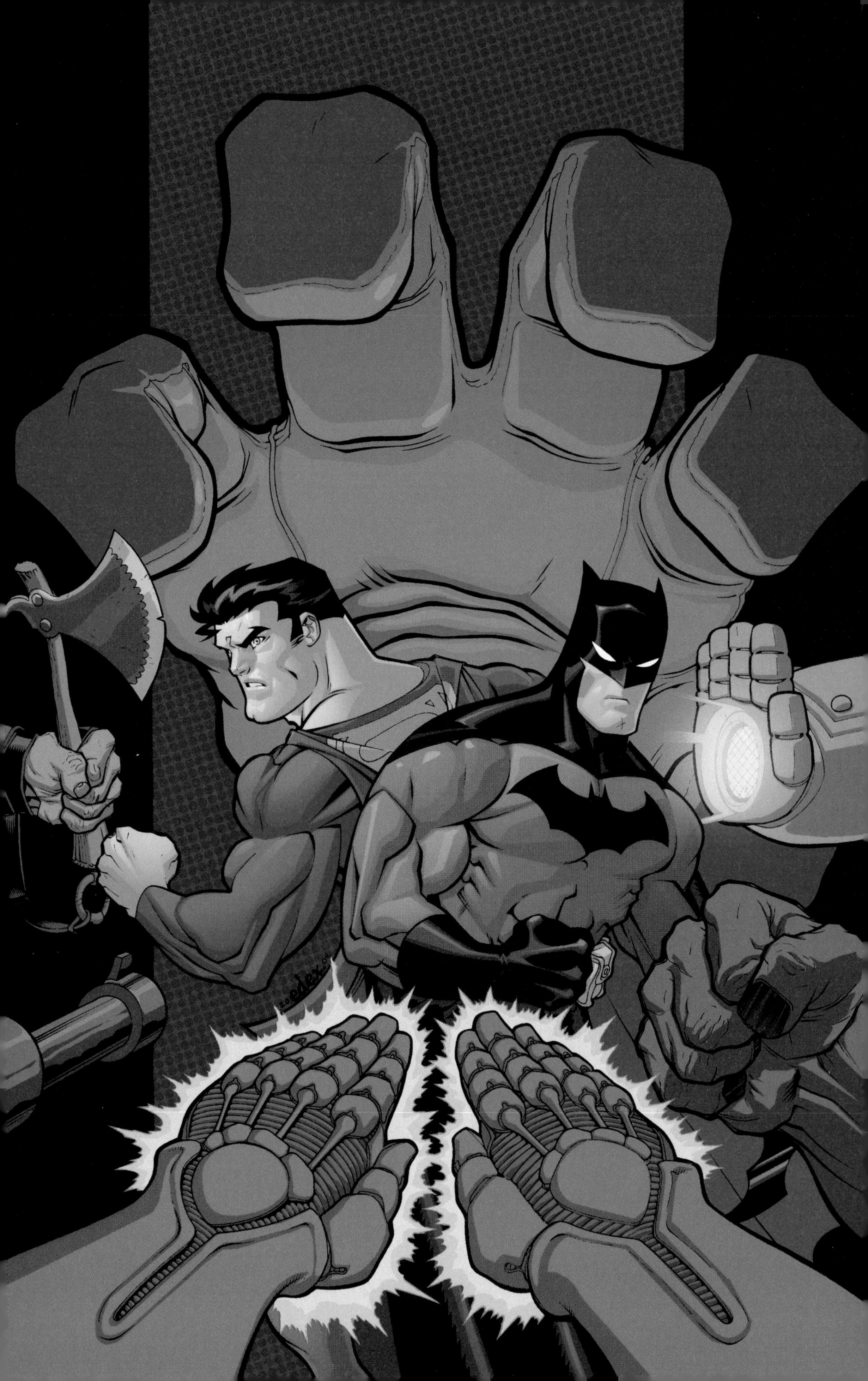

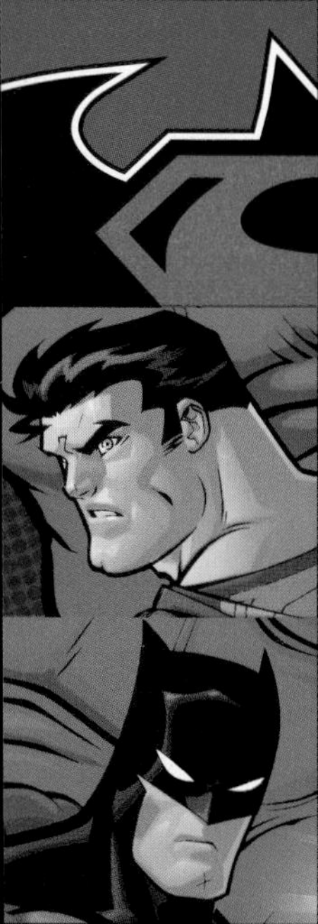

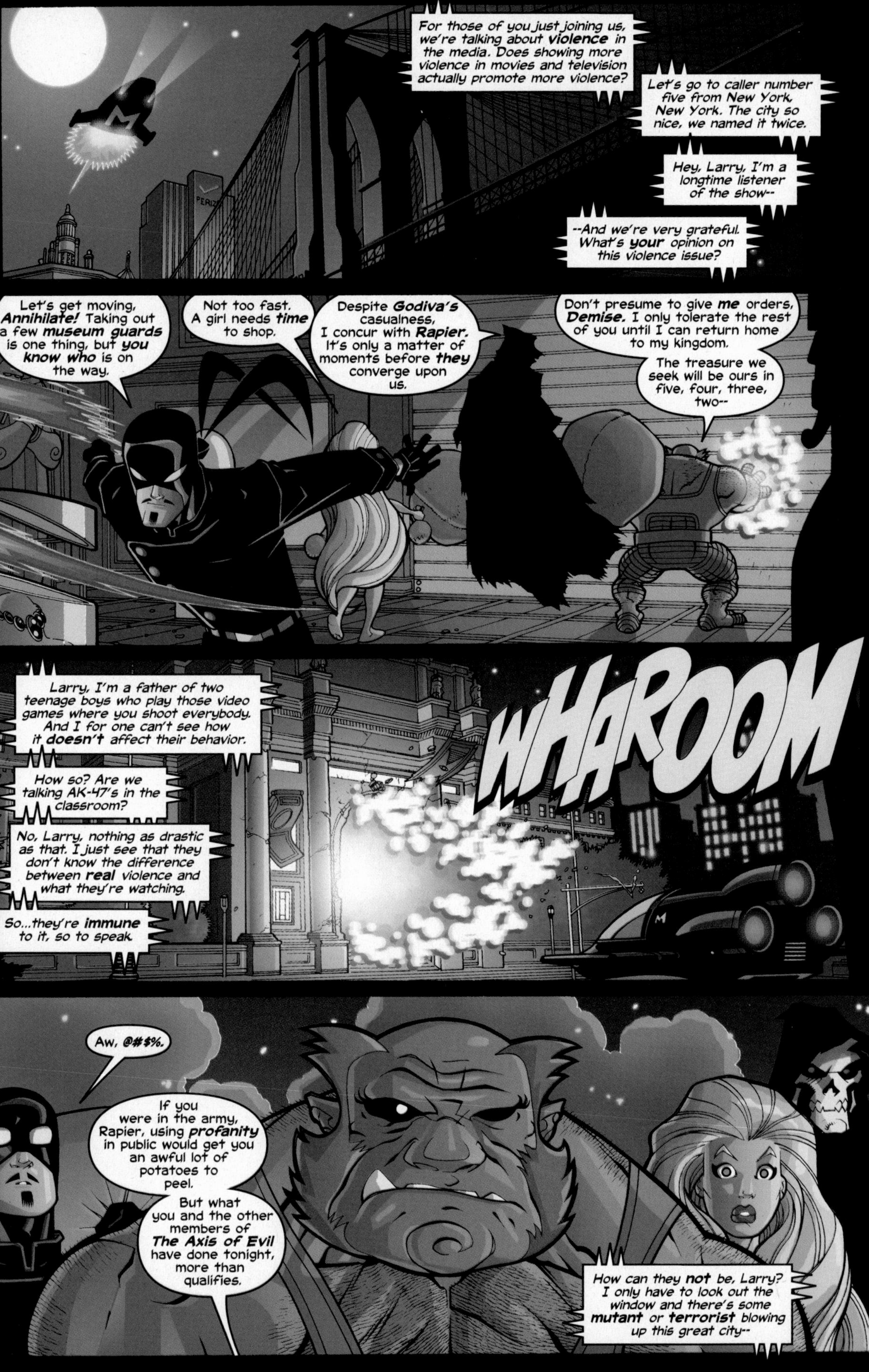
For those of you just joining us, we're talking about violence in the media. Does showing more violence in movies and television actually promote more violence?
Let's go to caller number five from New York, New York. The city so nice, we named it twice.
Hey, Larry, I'm a longtime listener of the show--
--And we're very grateful. What's your opinion on this violence issue?
PERIZ
Let's get moving, Annihilate! Taking out a few museum guards is one thing, but you know who is on the way.
Not too fast. A girl needs time to shop.
Despite Godiva's casualness, I concur with Rapier. It's only a matter of moments before they converge upon us.
Don't presume to give me orders, Demise. I only tolerate the rest of you until I can return home to my kingdom.
The treasure we seek will be ours in five, four, three, two--
Larry, I'm a father of two teenage boys who play those video games where you shoot everybody. And I for one can't see how it doesn't affect their behavior.
How so? Are we talking AK-47's in the classroom?
No, Larry, nothing as drastic as that. I just see that they don't know the difference between real violence and what they're watching.
So...they're immune to it, so to speak.
WHAROOM
Aw, @#$%.
If you were in the army, Rapier, using profanity in public would get you an awful lot of potatoes to peel.
But what you and the other members of The Axis of Evil have done tonight, more than qualifies.
How can they not be, Larry? I only have to look out the window and there's some mutant or terrorist blowing up this great city--

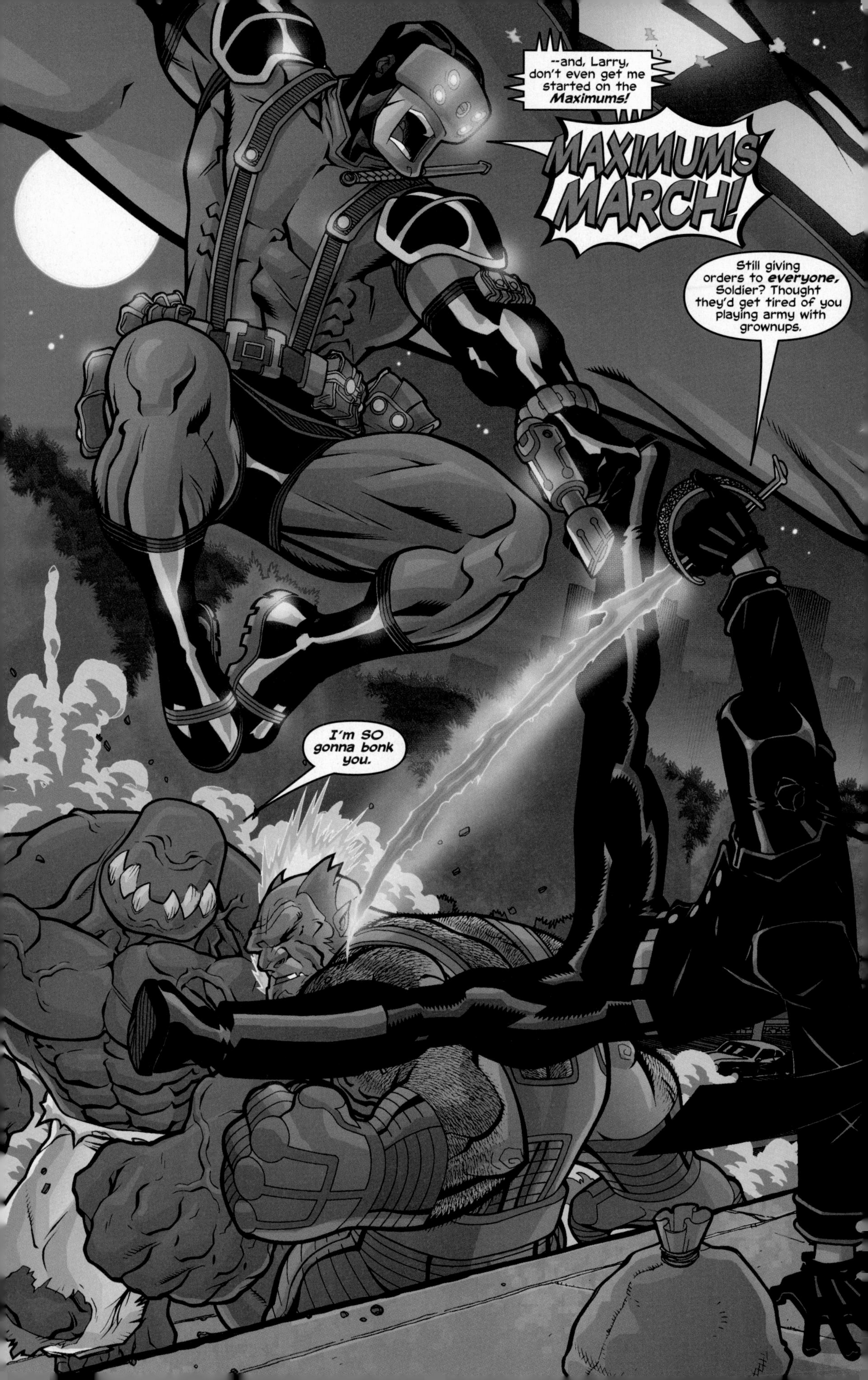
--and, Larry, don't even get me started on the *Maximums!*
MAXIMUMS MARCH!
Still giving orders to *everyone,* Soldier? Thought they'd get tired of you playing army with grownups.
I'm SO gonna bonk you.

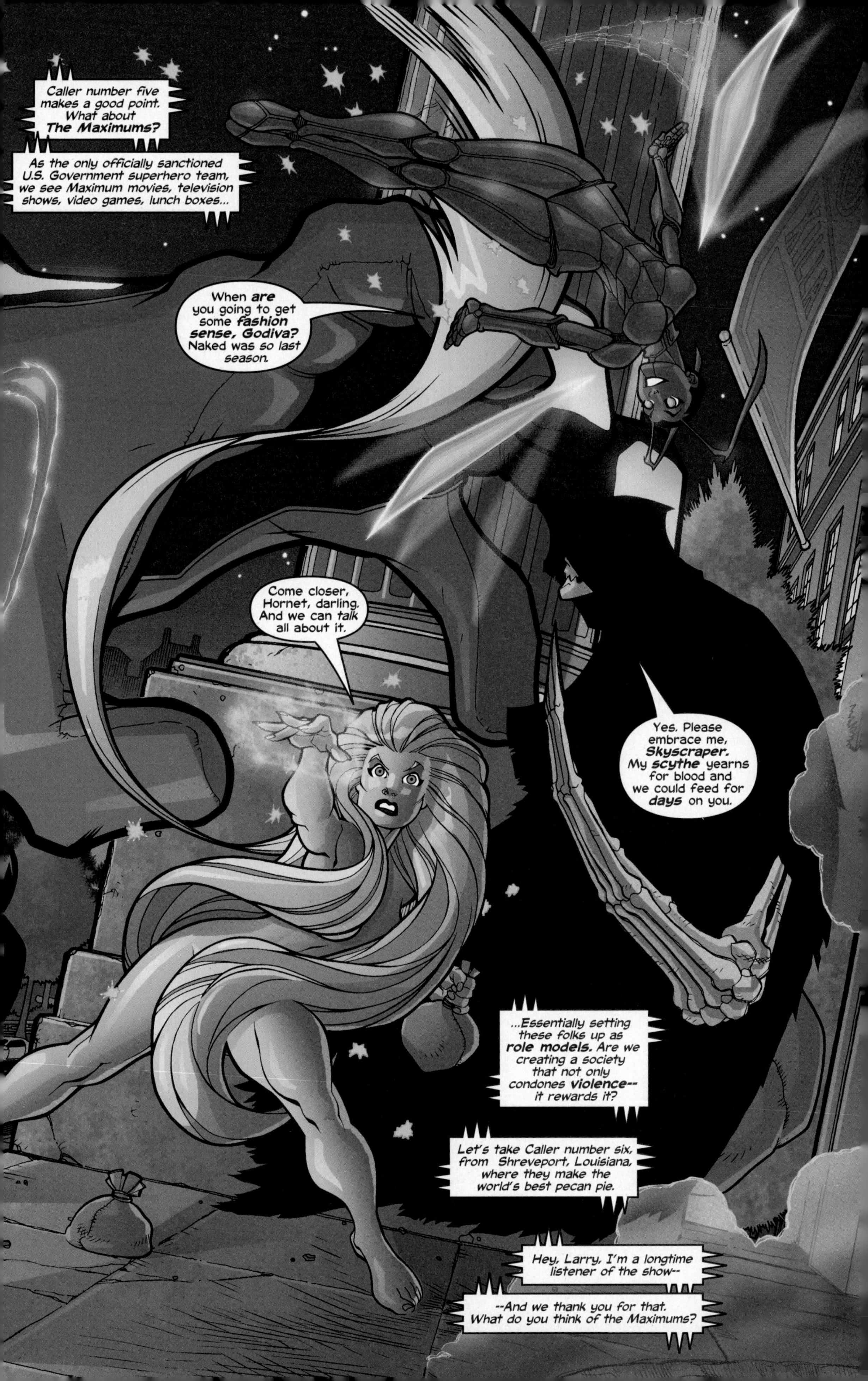
Caller number five makes a good point. What about The Maximums?
As the only officially sanctioned U.S. Government superhero team, we see Maximum movies, television shows, video games, lunch boxes...
When are you going to get some fashion sense, Godiva? Naked was so last season.
Come closer, Hornet, darling. And we can talk all about it.
Yes. Please embrace me, Skyscraper. My scythe yearns for blood and we could feed for days on you.
...Essentially setting these folks up as role models. Are we creating a society that not only condones violence-- it rewards it?
Let's take Caller number six, from Shreveport, Louisiana, where they make the world's best pecan pie.
Hey, Larry, I'm a longtime listener of the show--
--And we thank you for that. What do you think of the Maximums?

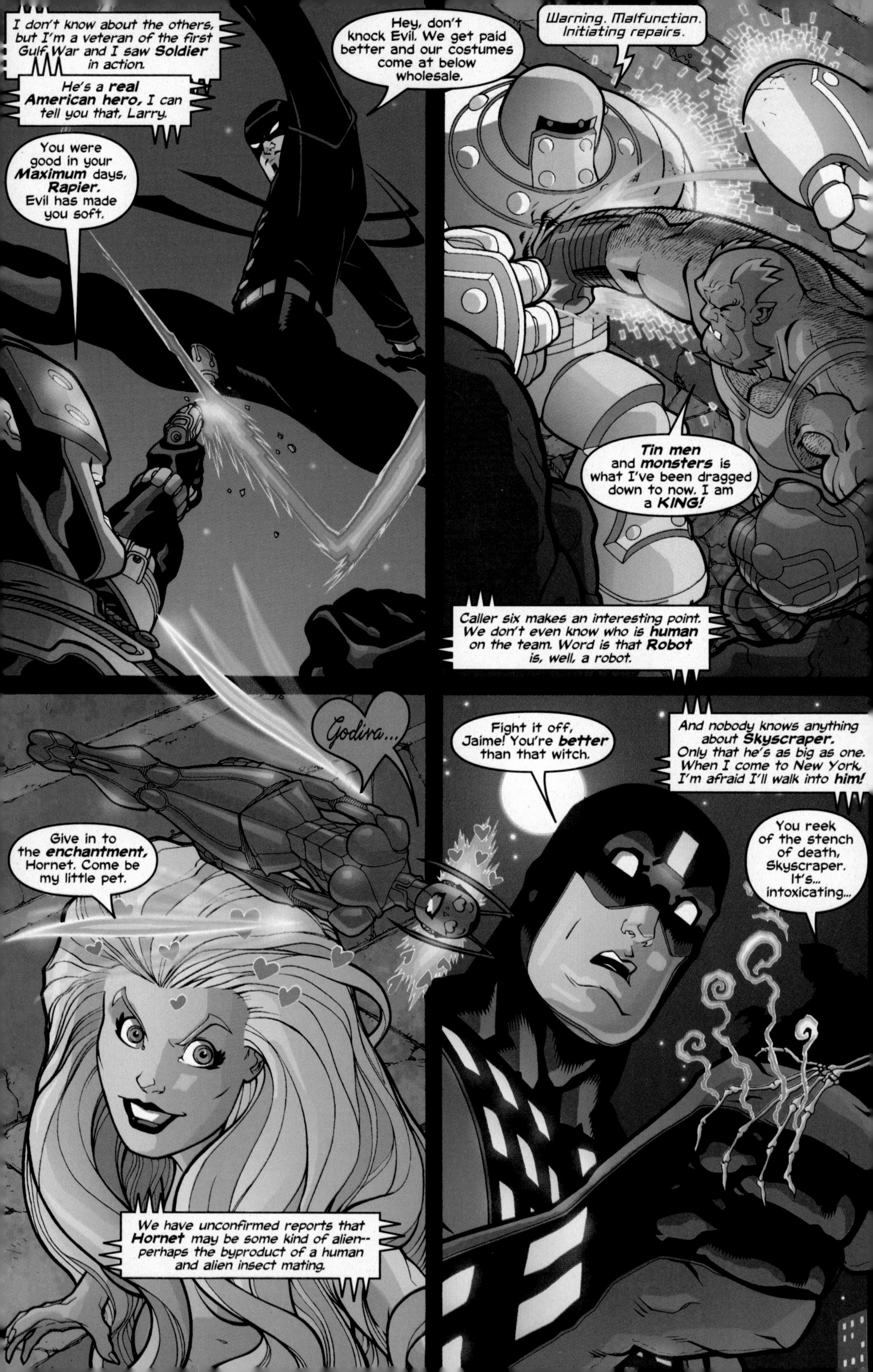
I don't know about the others, but I'm a veteran of the first Gulf War and I saw Soldier in action.
He's a real American hero, I can tell you that, Larry.
You were good in your Maximum days, Rapier. Evil has made you soft.
Hey, don't knock Evil. We get paid better and our costumes come at below wholesale.
Warning. Malfunction. Initiating repairs.
Tin men and monsters is what I've been dragged down to now. I am a KING!
Caller six makes an interesting point. We don't even know who is human on the team. Word is that Robot is, well, a robot.
Godiva...
Give in to the enchantment, Hornet. Come be my little pet.
We have unconfirmed reports that Hornet may be some kind of alien--perhaps the byproduct of a human and alien insect mating.
Fight it off, Jaime! You're better than that witch.
And nobody knows anything about Skyscraper. Only that he's as big as one. When I come to New York, I'm afraid I'll walk into him!
You reek of the stench of death, Skyscraper. It's... intoxicating...

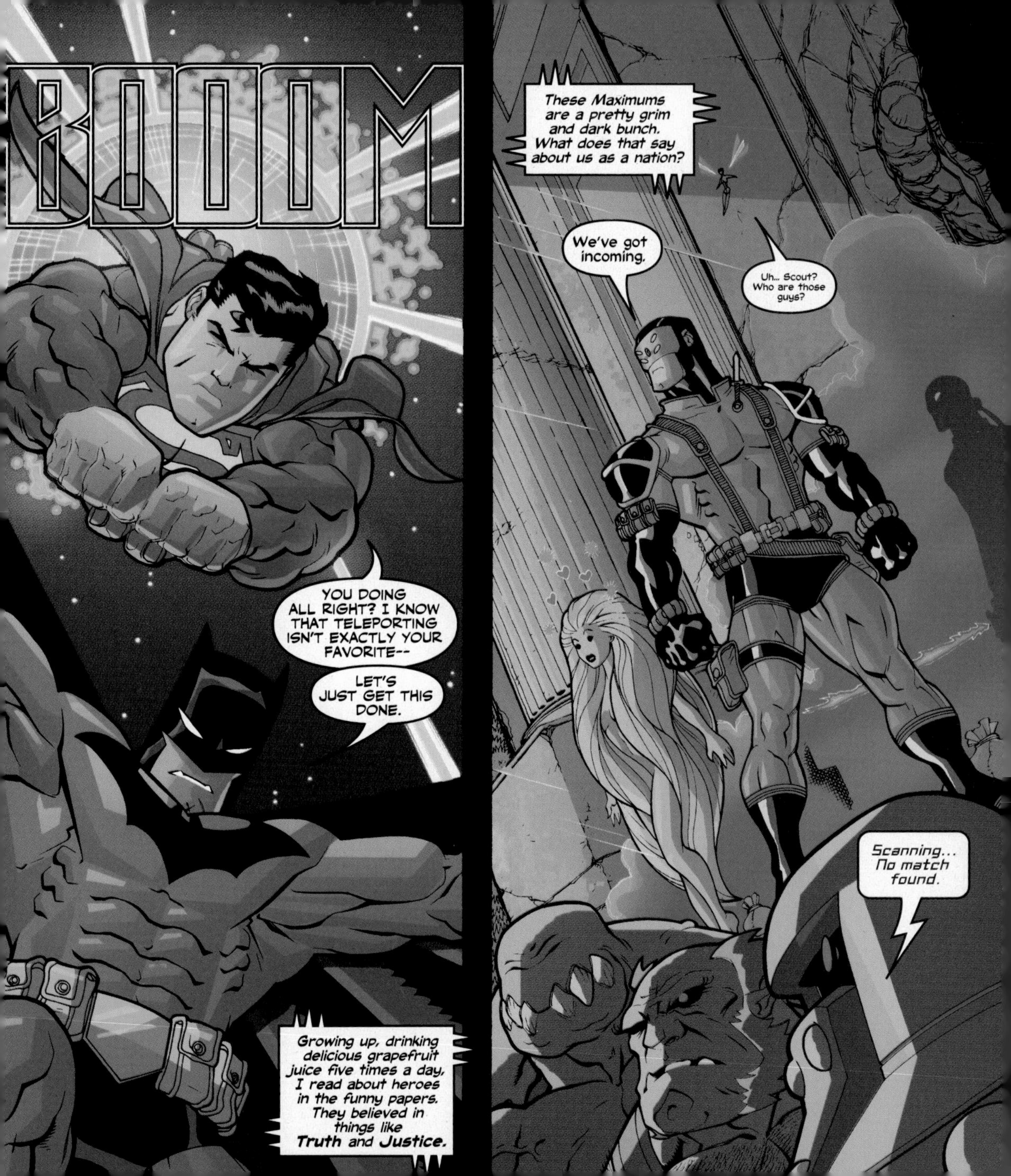
BOOOM
YOU DOING ALL RIGHT? I KNOW THAT TELEPORTING ISN'T EXACTLY YOUR FAVORITE--
LET'S JUST GET THIS DONE.
Growing up, drinking delicious grapefruit juice five times a day, I read about heroes in the funny papers. They believed in things like Truth and Justice.
These Maximums are a pretty grim and dark bunch. What does that say about us as a nation?
We've got incoming.
Uh... Scout? Who are those guys?
Scanning... No match found.

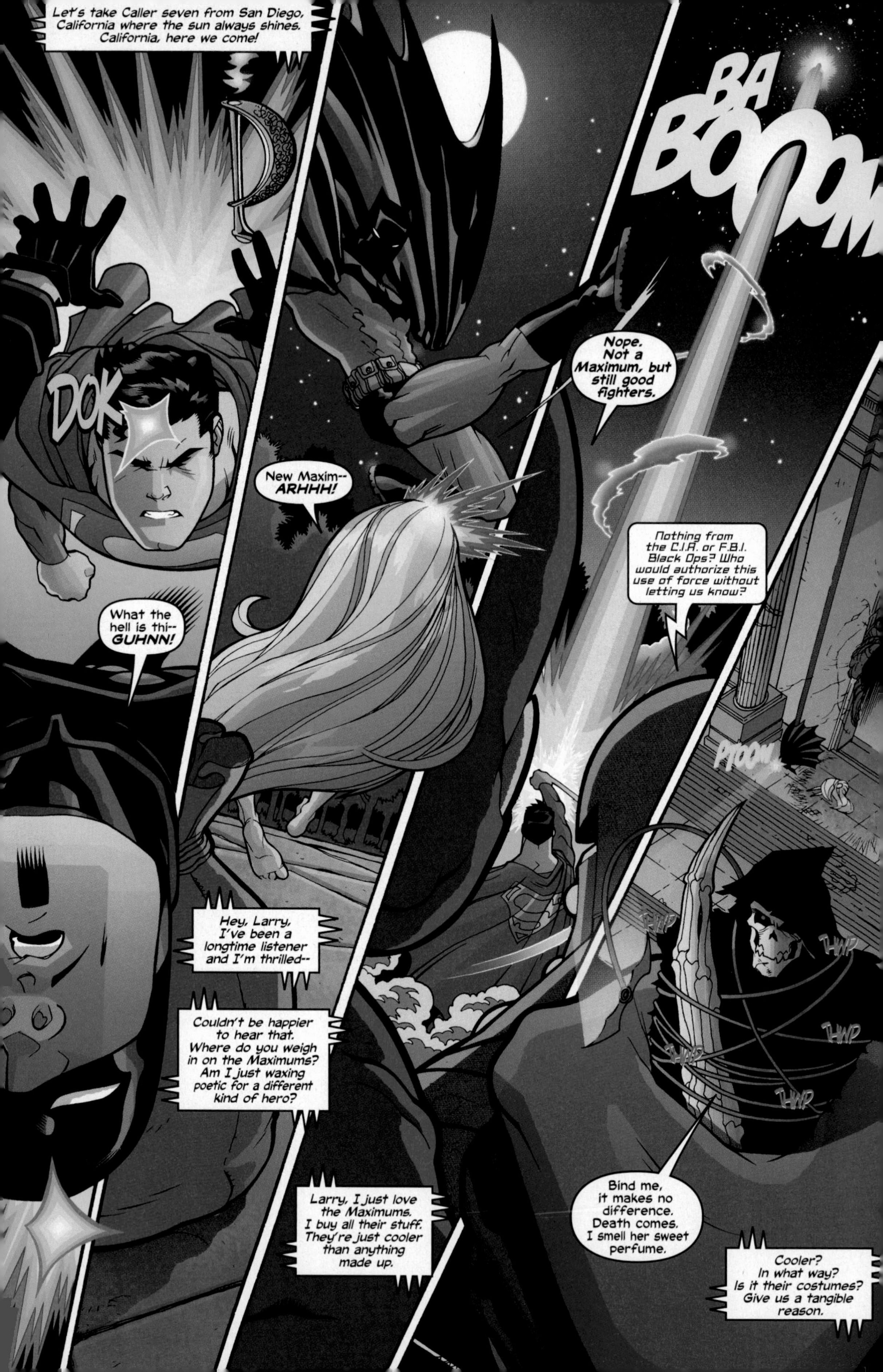
Let's take Caller seven from San Diego, California where the sun always shines. California, here we come!
DOK
What the hell is thi-- GUHNN!
New Maxim-- ARHHH!
BA BOOOM
Nope. Not a Maximum, but still good fighters.
Nothing from the C.I.A. or F.B.I. Black Ops? Who would authorize this use of force without letting us know?
PTOOM
Hey, Larry, I've been a longtime listener and I'm thrilled--
Couldn't be happier to hear that. Where do you weigh in on the Maximums? Am I just waxing poetic for a different kind of hero?
THWP
THWP
THWP
THWP
THWP
Bind me, it makes no difference. Death comes. I smell her sweet perfume.
Larry, I just love the Maximums. I buy all their stuff. They're just cooler than anything made up.
Cooler? In what way? Is it their costumes? Give us a tangible reason.

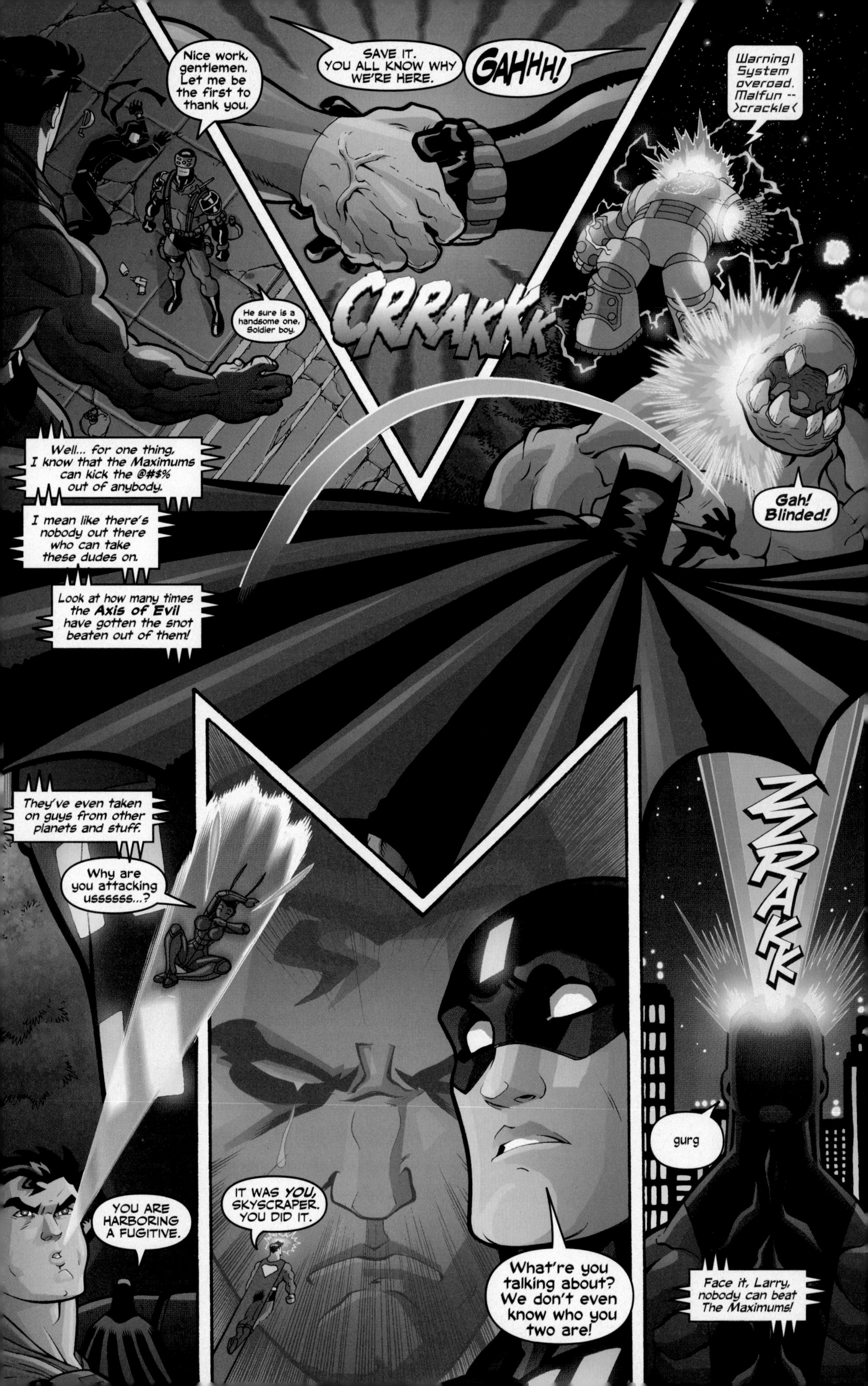
Nice work, gentlemen. Let me be the first to thank you.
SAVE IT. YOU ALL KNOW WHY WE'RE HERE.
GAHHH!
Warning! System overoad. Malfun -- >crackle<
He sure is a handsome one, Soldier boy.
CRRAKKK
Well... for one thing, I know that the Maximums can kick the @#$% out of anybody.
I mean like there's nobody out there who can take these dudes on.
Look at how many times the Axis of Evil have gotten the snot beaten out of them!
Gah! Blinded!
They've even taken on guys from other planets and stuff.
Why are you attacking ussssss...?
ZZRAKK
gurg
YOU ARE HARBORING A FUGITIVE.
IT WAS YOU, SKYSCRAPER. YOU DID IT.
What're you talking about? We don't even know who you two are!
Face it, Larry, nobody can beat The Maximums!

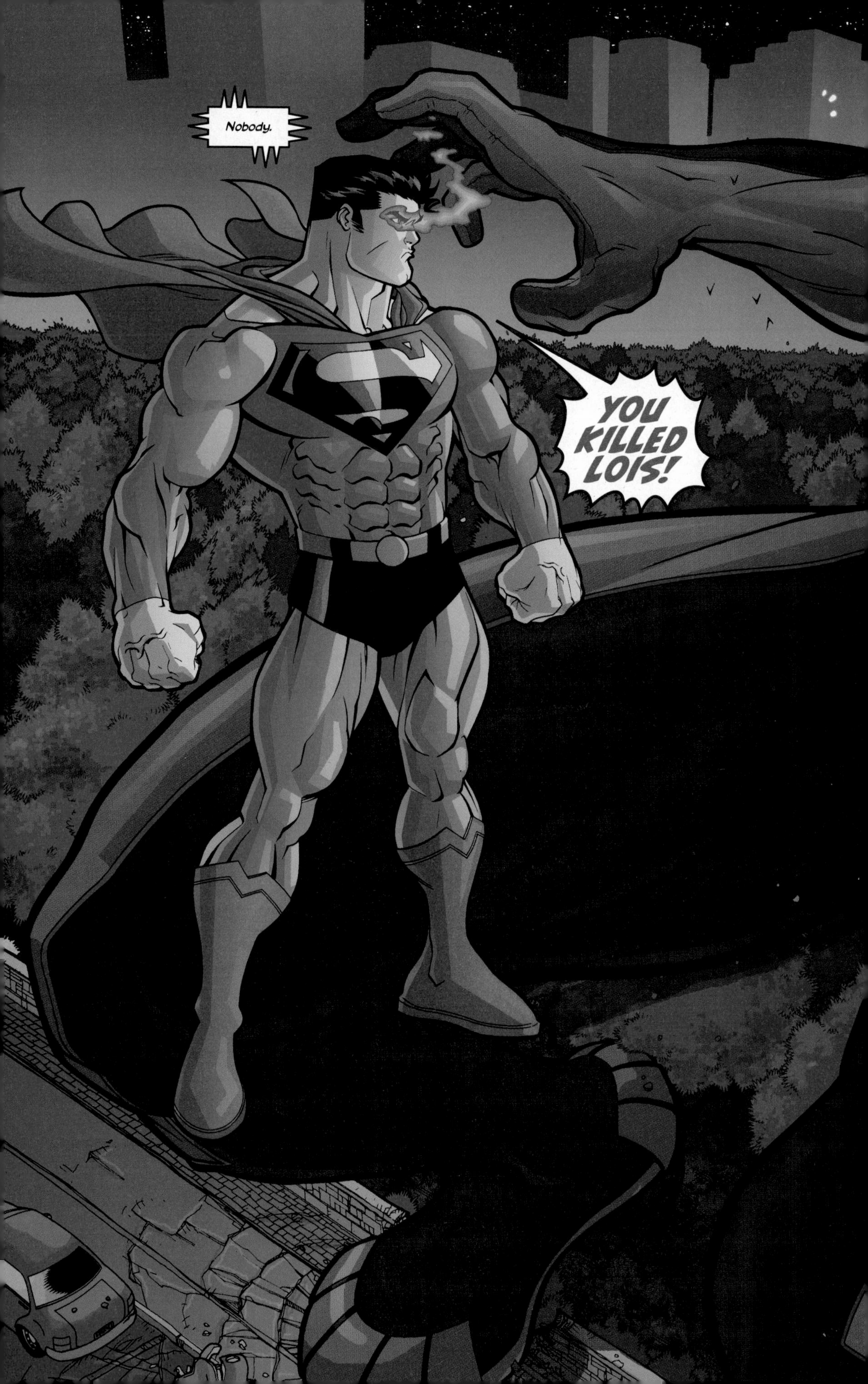
Nobody.
YOU KILLED LOIS!

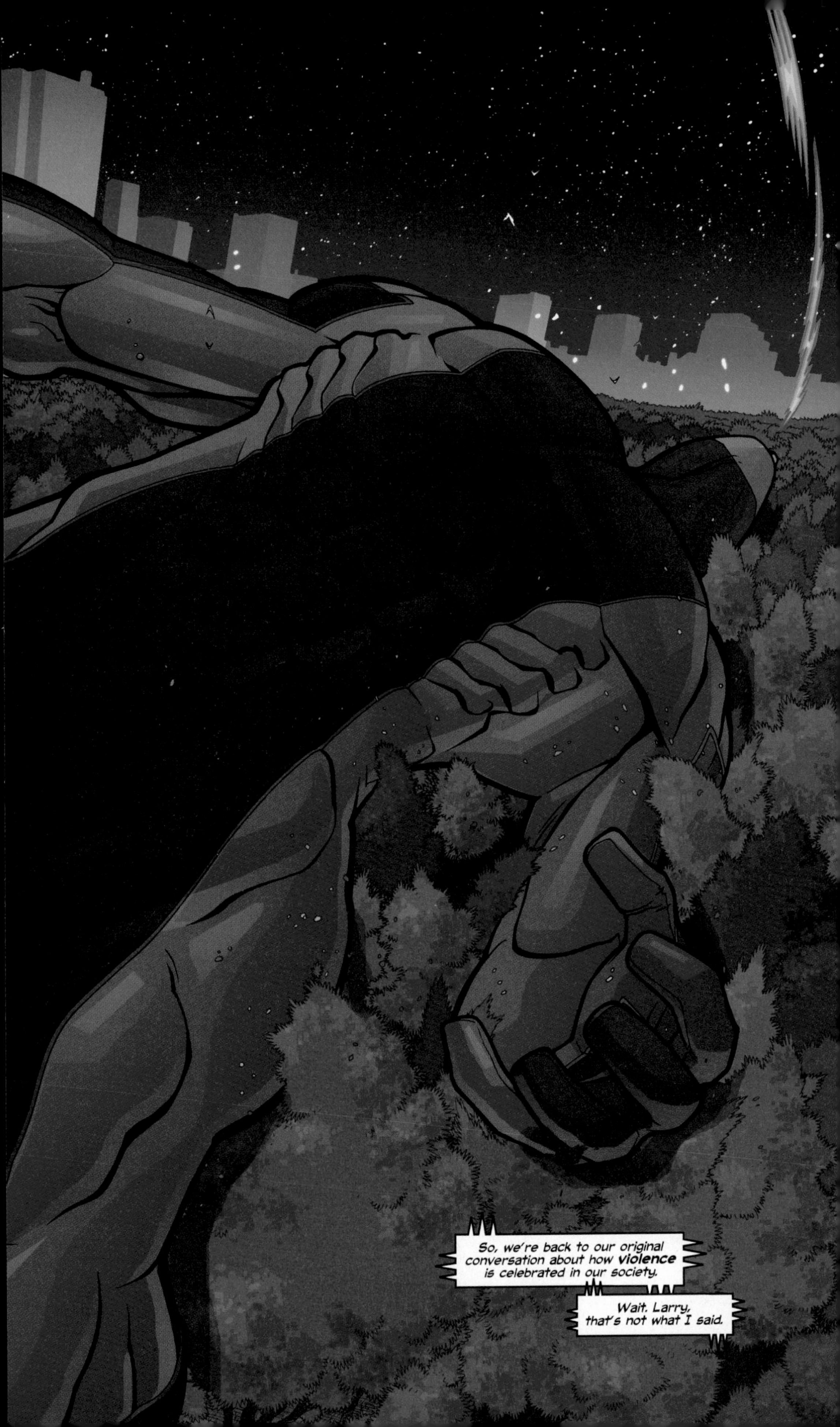
So, we're back to our original conversation about how **violence** is celebrated in our society.
Wait, Larry, that's not what I said.

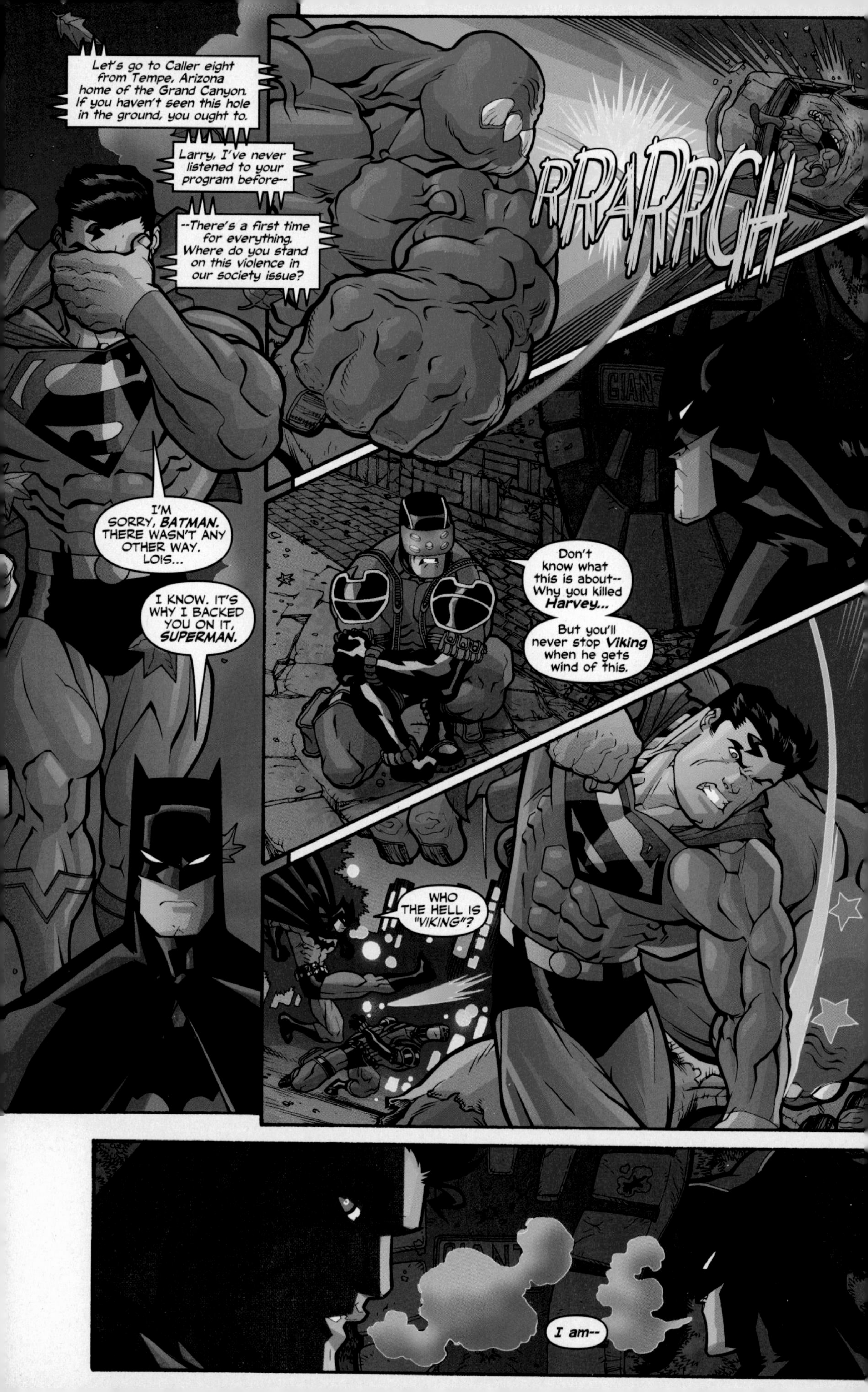
Let's go to Caller eight from Tempe, Arizona home of the Grand Canyon. If you haven't seen this hole in the ground, you ought to.
Larry, I've never listened to your program before--
--There's a first time for everything. Where do you stand on this violence in our society issue?
RRARRGH
I'M SORRY, BATMAN. THERE WASN'T ANY OTHER WAY. LOIS...
I KNOW. IT'S WHY I BACKED YOU ON IT, SUPERMAN.
Don't know what this is about-- Why you killed Harvey...
But you'll never stop Viking when he gets wind of this.
WHO THE HELL IS "VIKING"?
I am--

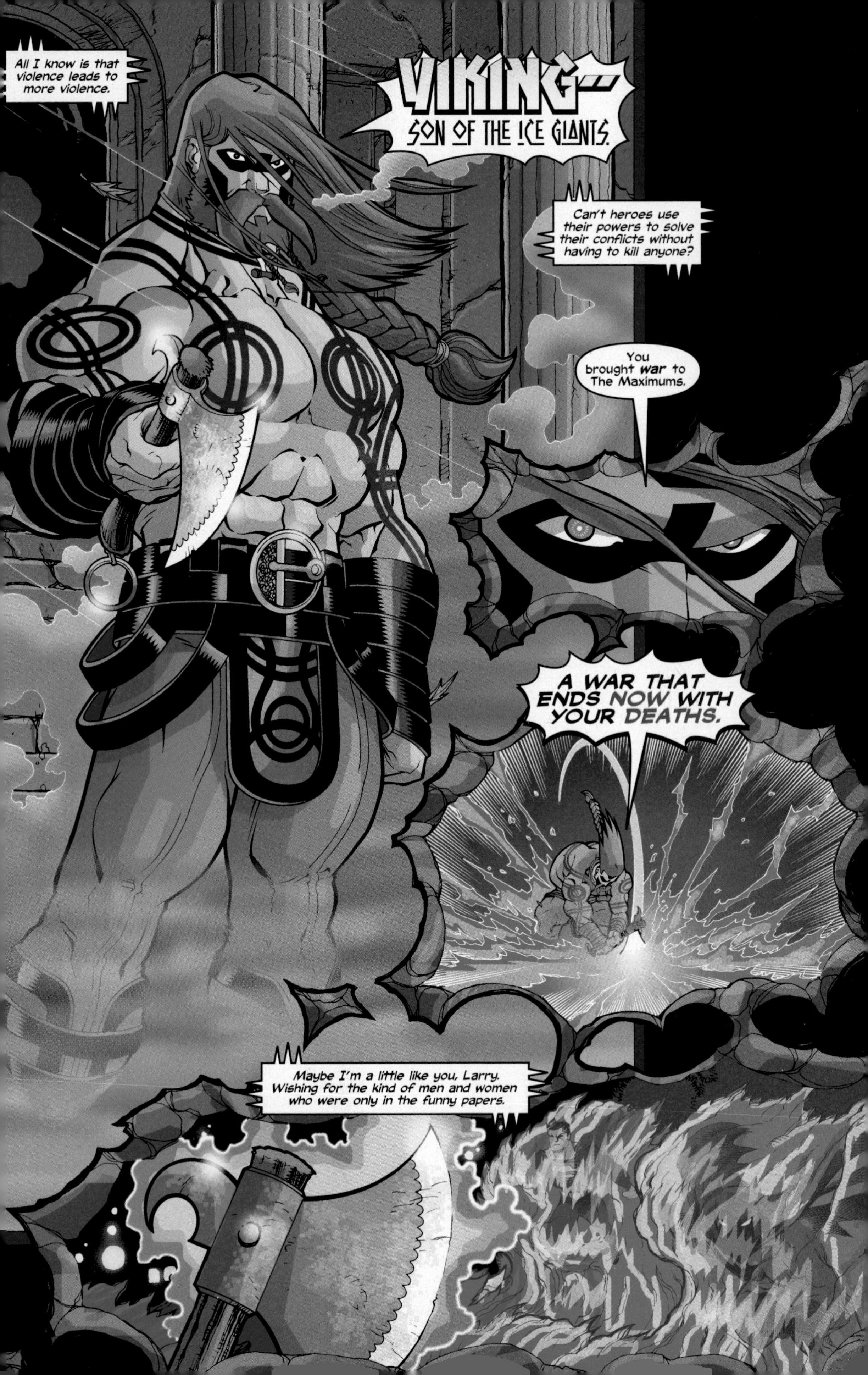
All I know is that violence leads to more violence.
VIKING — SON OF THE ICE GIANTS.
Can't heroes use their powers to solve their conflicts without having to kill anyone?
You brought war to The Maximums.
A WAR THAT ENDS NOW WITH YOUR DEATHS.
Maybe I'm a little like you, Larry. Wishing for the kind of men and women who were only in the funny papers.

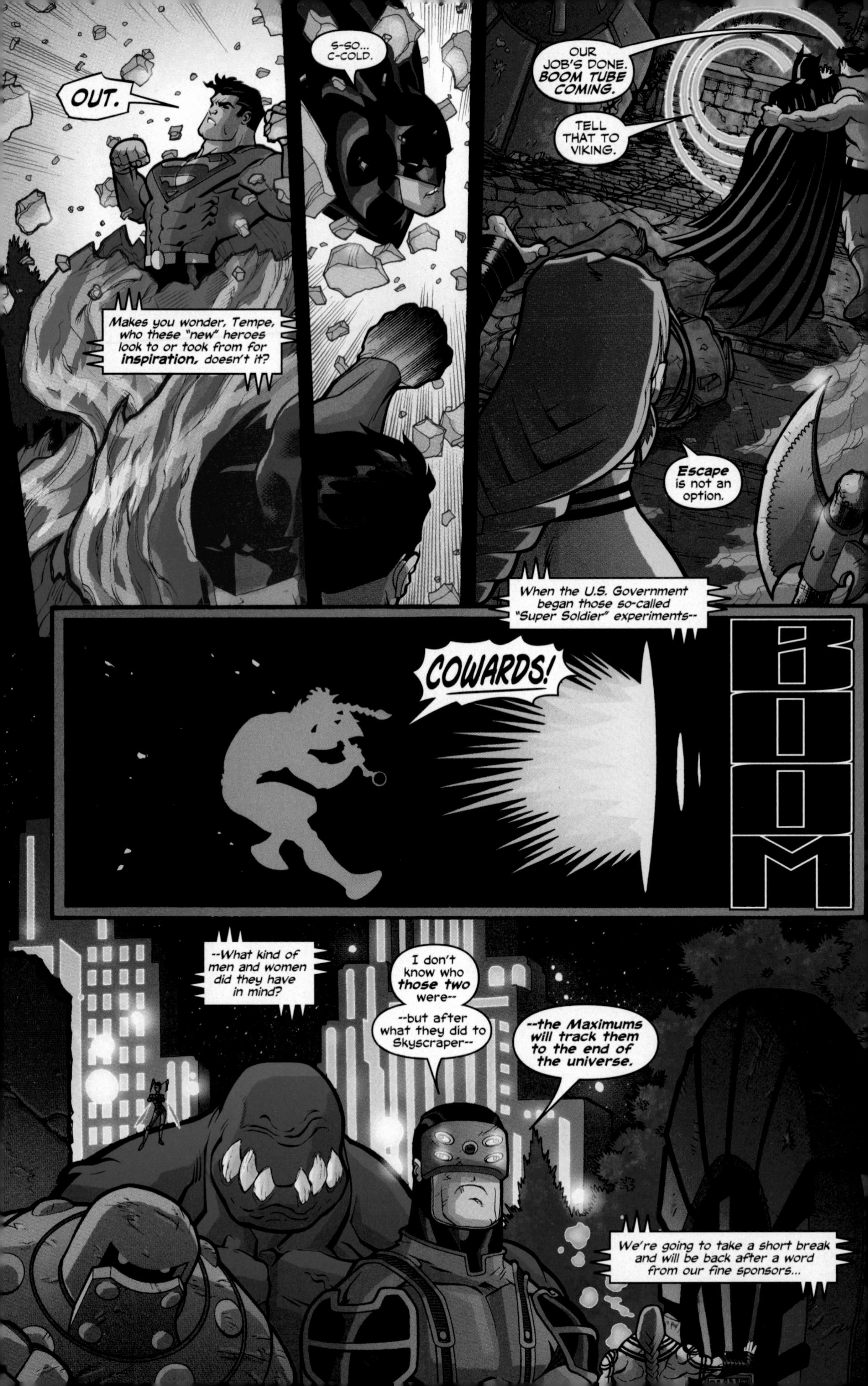
OUT.
Makes you wonder, Tempe, who these "new" heroes look to or took from for inspiration, doesn't it?
S-SO... C-COLD.
OUR JOB'S DONE. BOOM TUBE COMING.
TELL THAT TO VIKING.
Escape is not an option.
When the U.S. Government began those so-called "Super Soldier" experiments--
COWARDS!
BOOM
--What kind of men and women did they have in mind?
I don't know who those two were--
--but after what they did to Skyscraper--
--the Maximums will track them to the end of the universe.
We're going to take a short break and will be back after a word from our fine sponsors...

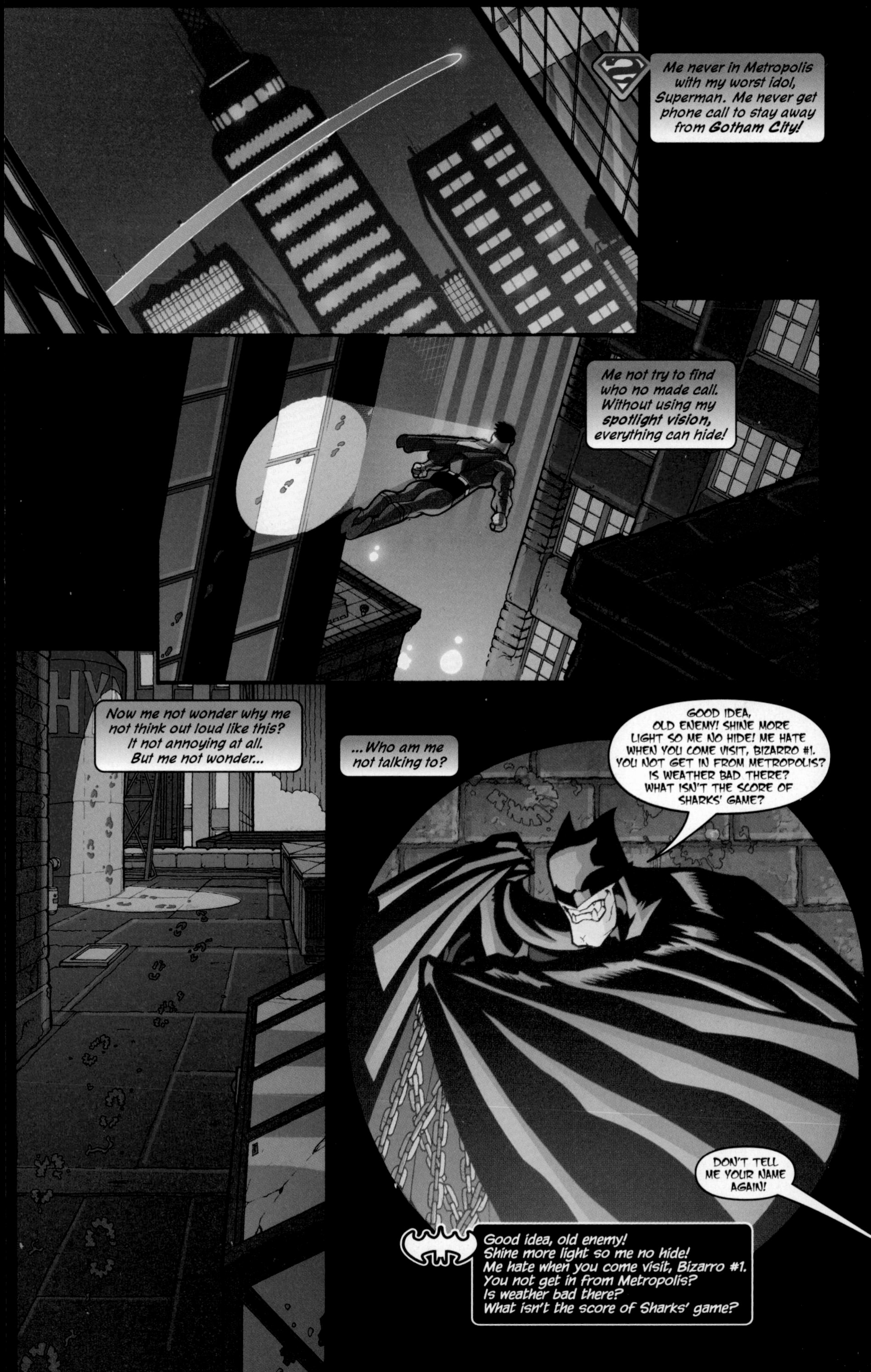

Me never in Metropolis with my worst idol, Superman. Me never get phone call to stay away from Gotham City!
Me not try to find who no made call. Without using my spotlight vision, everything can hide!
Now me not wonder why me not think out loud like this? It not annoying at all. But me not wonder...
...Who am me not talking to?
GOOD IDEA, OLD ENEMY! SHINE MORE LIGHT SO ME NO HIDE! ME HATE WHEN YOU COME VISIT, BIZARRO #1. YOU NOT GET IN FROM METROPOLIS? IS WEATHER BAD THERE? WHAT ISN'T THE SCORE OF SHARKS' GAME?
DON'T TELL ME YOUR NAME AGAIN!
Good idea, old enemy!
Shine more light so me no hide!
Me hate when you come visit, Bizarro #1.
You not get in from Metropolis?
Is weather bad there?
What isn't the score of Sharks' game?

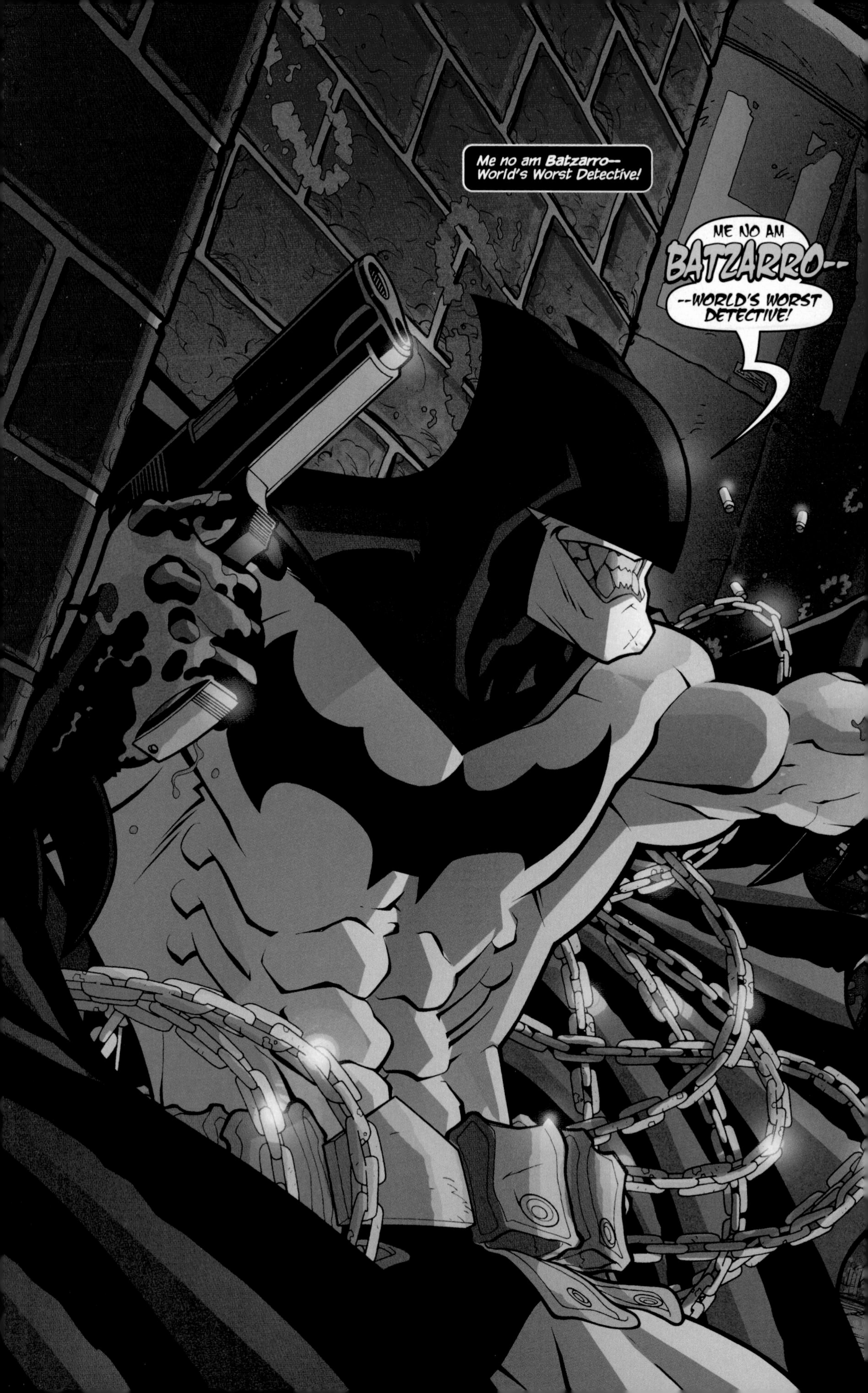
Me no am Batzarro--
World's Worst Detective!
ME NO AM BATZARRO--
--WORLD'S WORST DETECTIVE!

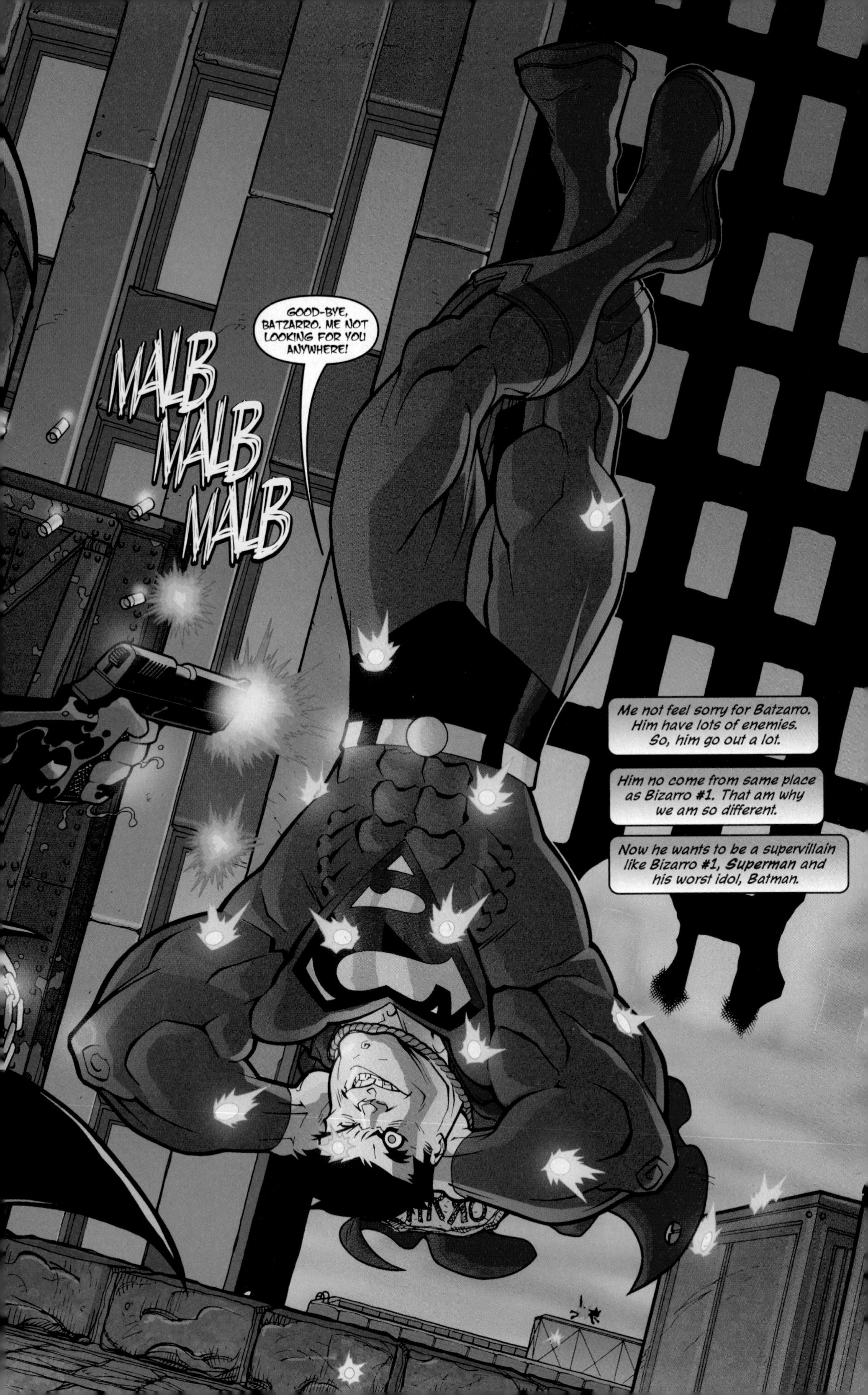
GOOD-BYE, BATZARRO. ME NOT LOOKING FOR YOU ANYWHERE!
MALB MALB MALB
Me not feel sorry for Batzarro. Him have lots of enemies. So, him go out a lot.
Him no come from same place as Bizarro #1. That am why we am so different.
Now he wants to be a supervillain like Bizarro #1, Superman and his worst idol, Batman.

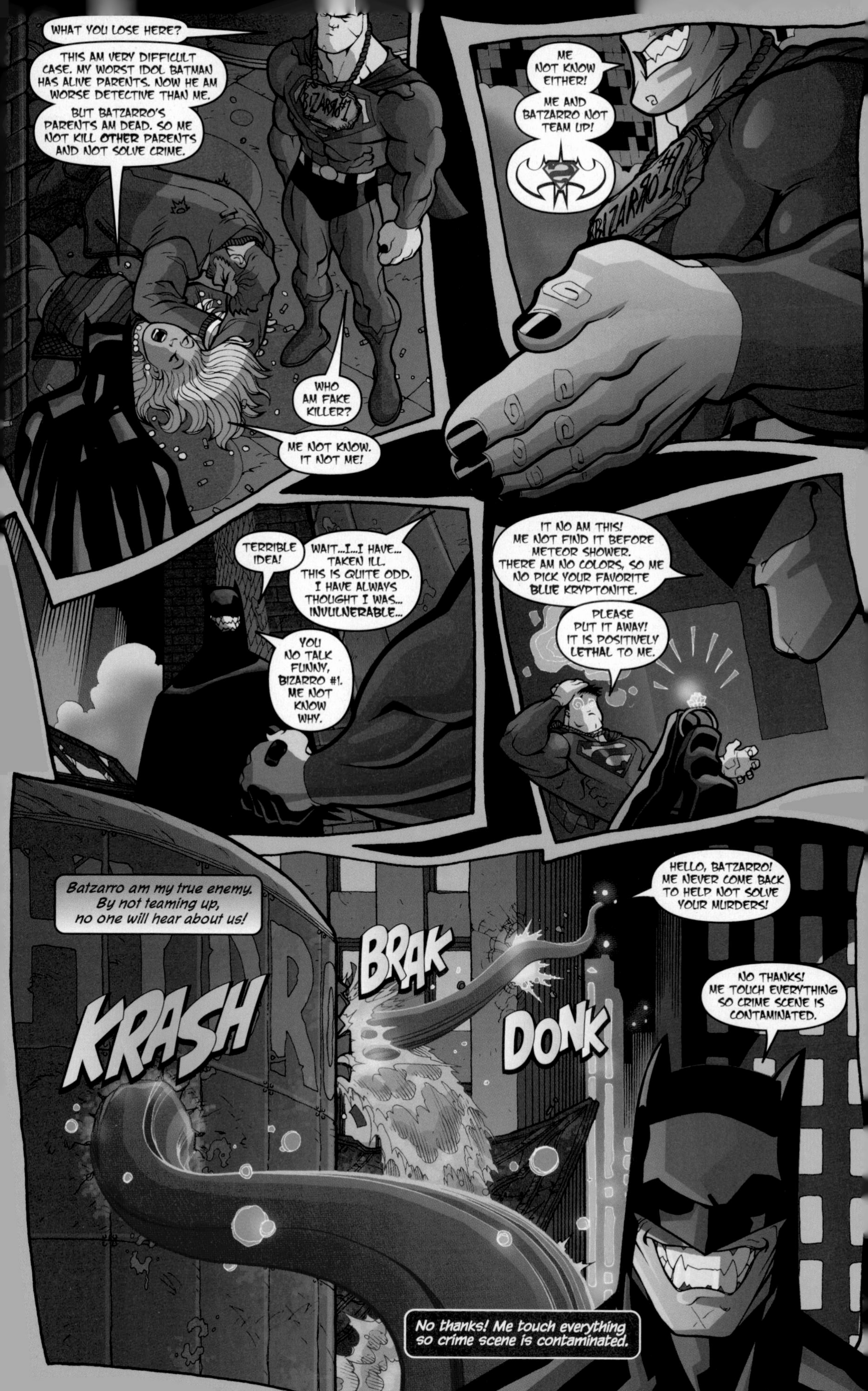
WHAT YOU LOSE HERE?
THIS AM VERY DIFFICULT CASE. MY WORST IDOL BATMAN HAS ALIVE PARENTS. NOW HE AM WORSE DETECTIVE THAN ME.
BUT BATZARRO'S PARENTS AM DEAD. SO ME NOT KILL OTHER PARENTS AND NOT SOLVE CRIME.
BIZARRO #1
WHO AM FAKE KILLER?
ME NOT KNOW. IT NOT ME!
ME NOT KNOW EITHER!
ME AND BATZARRO NOT TEAM UP!
TERRIBLE IDEA!
WAIT...I...I HAVE... TAKEN ILL. THIS IS QUITE ODD. I HAVE ALWAYS THOUGHT I WAS... INVULNERABLE...
YOU NO TALK FUNNY, BIZARRO #1. ME NOT KNOW WHY.
IT NO AM THIS! ME NOT FIND IT BEFORE METEOR SHOWER. THERE AM NO COLORS, SO ME NO PICK YOUR FAVORITE BLUE KRYPTONITE.
PLEASE PUT IT AWAY! IT IS POSITIVELY LETHAL TO ME.
Batzarro am my true enemy. By not teaming up, no one will hear about us!
KRASH
BRAK
DONK
HELLO, BATZARRO! ME NEVER COME BACK TO HELP NOT SOLVE YOUR MURDERS!
NO THANKS! ME TOUCH EVERYTHING SO CRIME SCENE IS CONTAMINATED.
No thanks! Me touch everything so crime scene is contaminated.

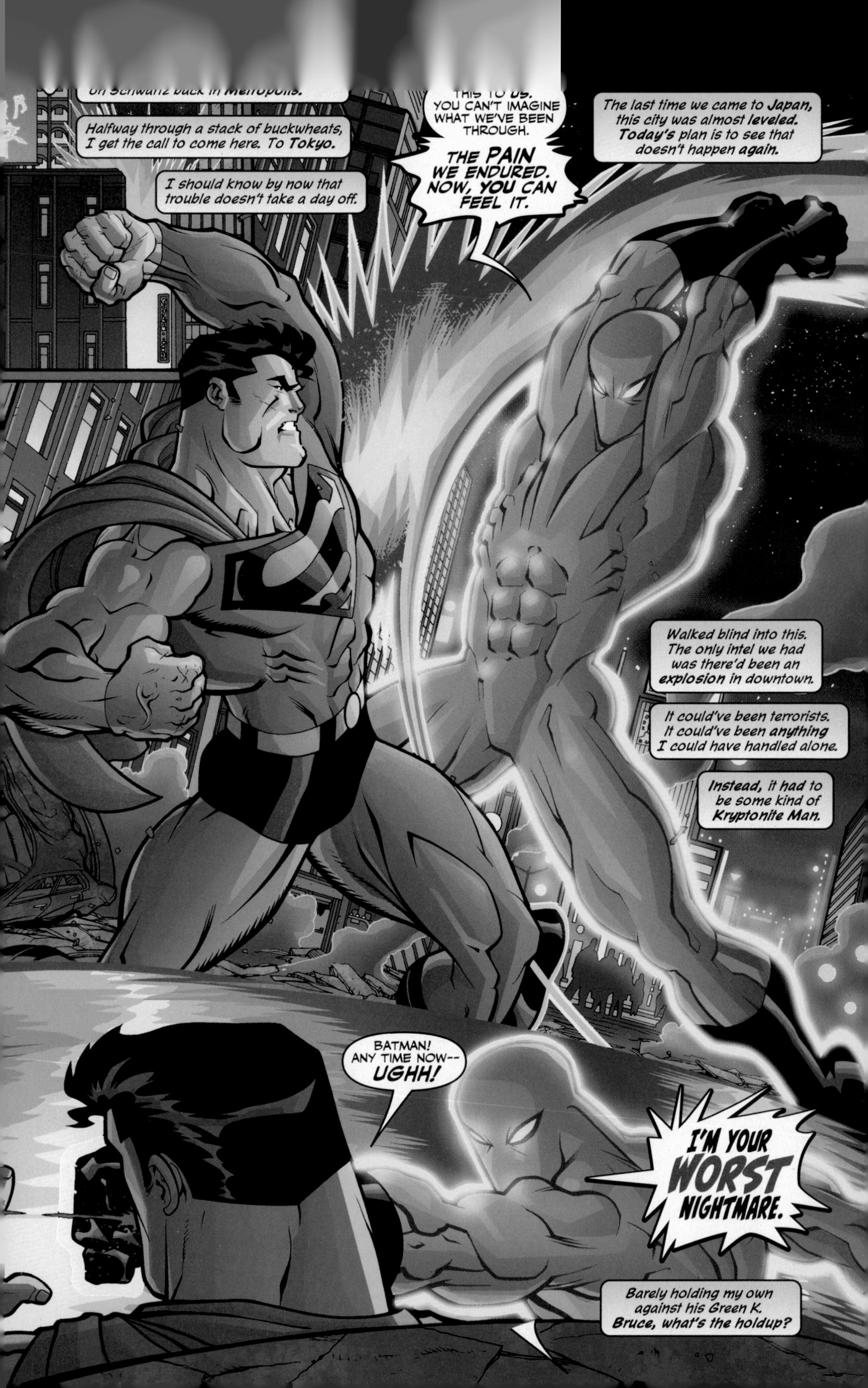
Halfway through a stack of buckwheats, I get the call to come here. To Tokyo.
I should know by now that trouble doesn't take a day off.
YOU CAN'T IMAGINE WHAT WE'VE BEEN THROUGH.
THE PAIN WE ENDURED. NOW, YOU CAN FEEL IT.
The last time we came to Japan, this city was almost leveled. Today's plan is to see that doesn't happen again.
Walked blind into this. The only intel we had was there'd been an explosion in downtown.
It could've been terrorists. It could've been anything I could have handled alone.
Instead, it had to be some kind of Kryptonite Man.
BATMAN! ANY TIME NOW-- UGHH!
I'M YOUR WORST NIGHTMARE.
Barely holding my own against his Green K. Bruce, what's the holdup?

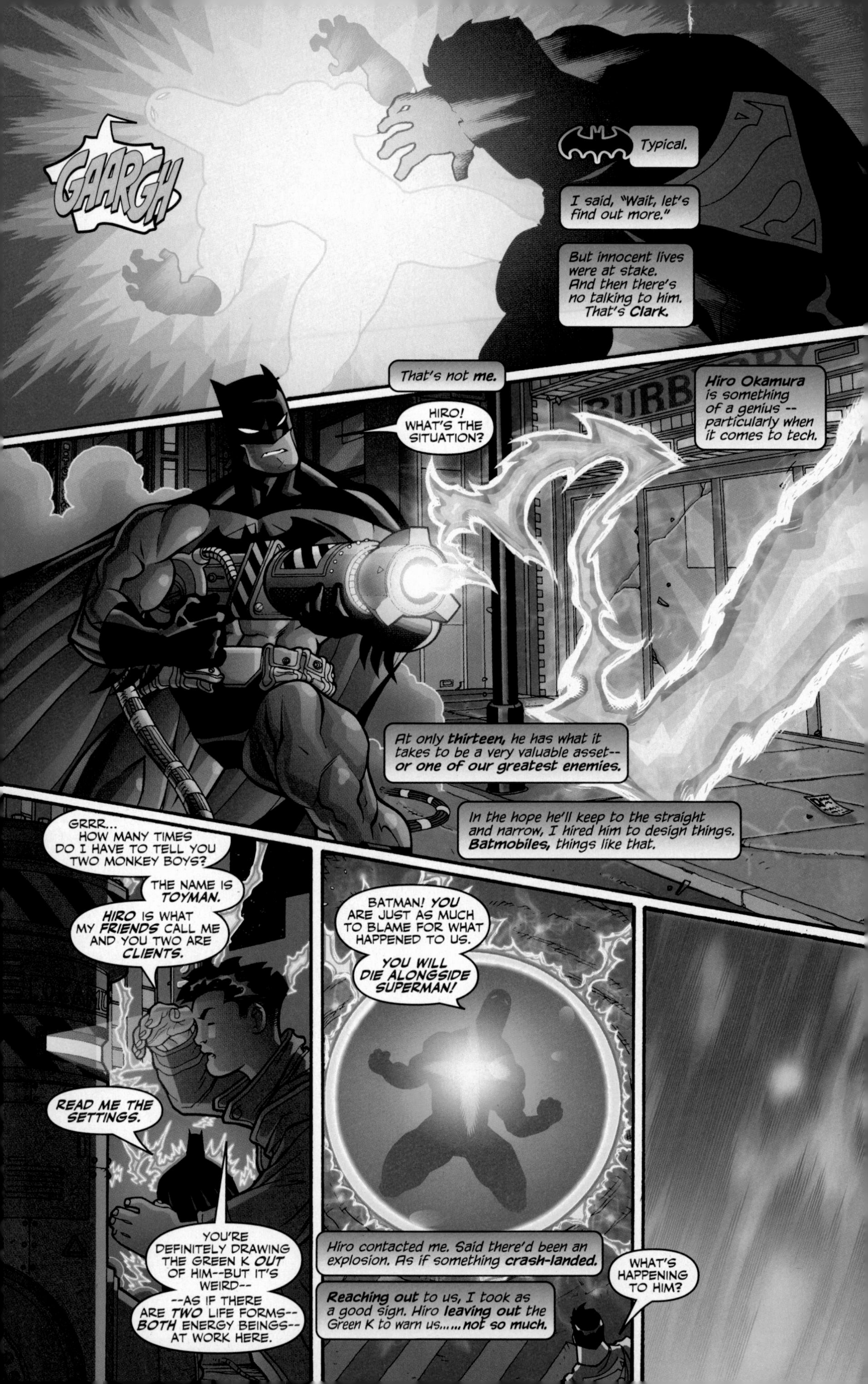

GAARGH
Typical.
I said, "Wait, let's find out more."
But innocent lives were at stake. And then there's no talking to him. That's Clark.
That's not me.
HIRO! WHAT'S THE SITUATION?
Hiro Okamura is something of a genius -- particularly when it comes to tech.
At only thirteen, he has what it takes to be a very valuable asset-- or one of our greatest enemies.
In the hope he'll keep to the straight and narrow, I hired him to design things. Batmobiles, things like that.
GRRR... HOW MANY TIMES DO I HAVE TO TELL YOU TWO MONKEY BOYS?
THE NAME IS TOYMAN.
HIRO IS WHAT MY FRIENDS CALL ME AND YOU TWO ARE CLIENTS.
READ ME THE SETTINGS.
YOU'RE DEFINITELY DRAWING THE GREEN K OUT OF HIM--BUT IT'S WEIRD--
--AS IF THERE ARE TWO LIFE FORMS-- BOTH ENERGY BEINGS-- AT WORK HERE.
BATMAN! YOU ARE JUST AS MUCH TO BLAME FOR WHAT HAPPENED TO US.
YOU WILL DIE ALONGSIDE SUPERMAN!
Hiro contacted me. Said there'd been an explosion. As if something crash-landed.
Reaching out to us, I took as a good sign. Hiro leaving out the Green K to warn us...... not so much.
WHAT'S HAPPENING TO HIM?

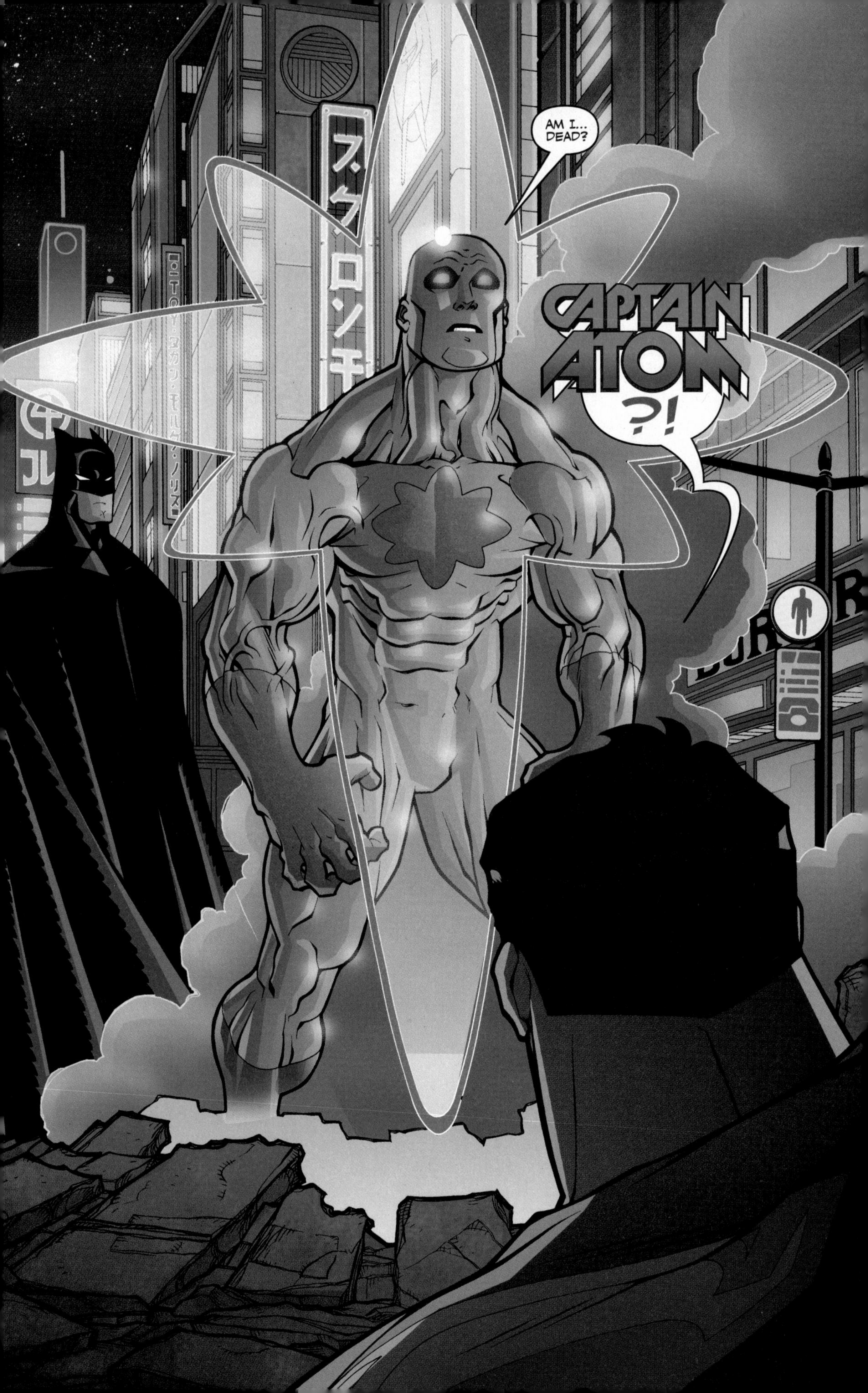
AM I... DEAD?
CAPTAIN ATOM ?!

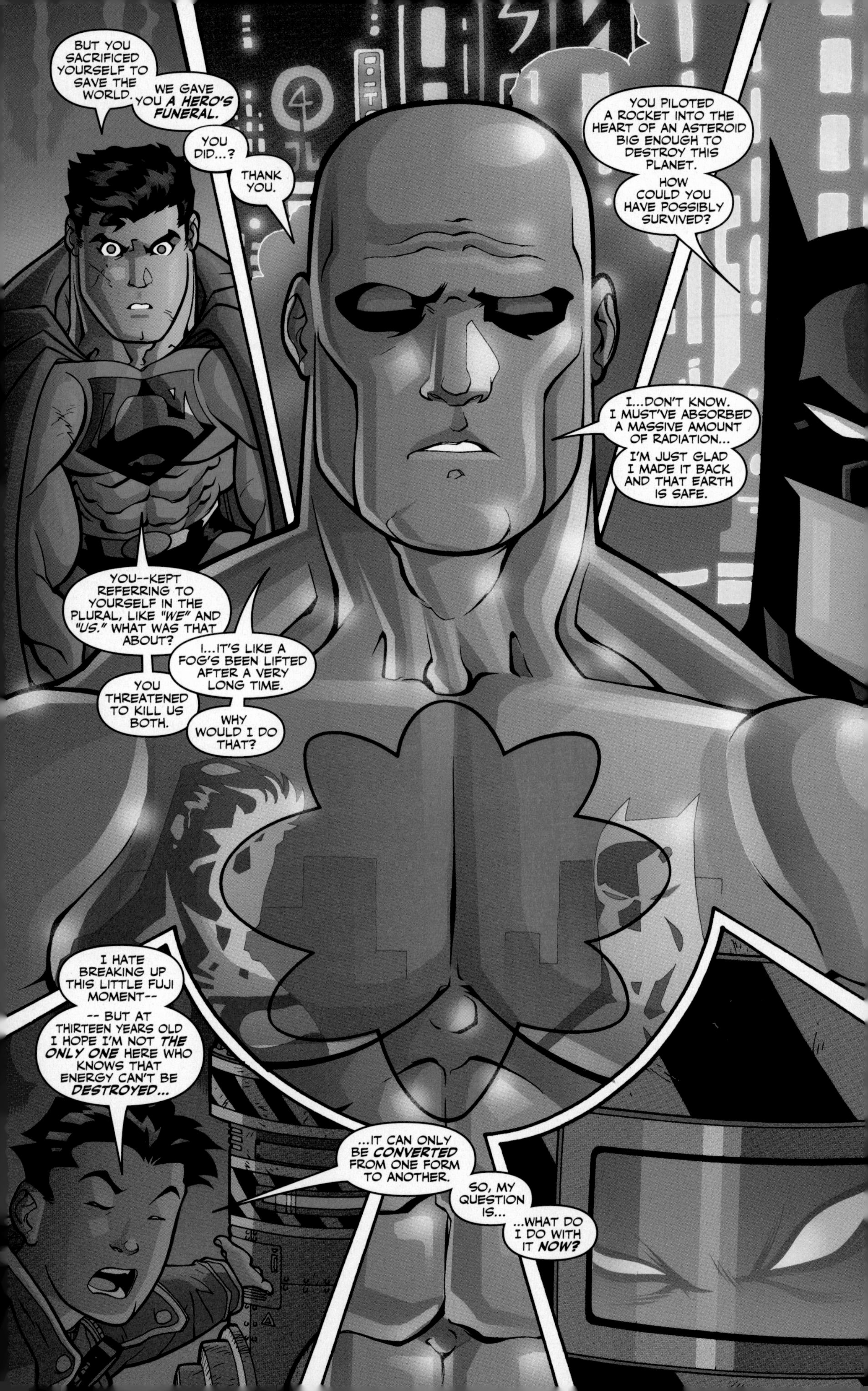
BUT YOU SACRIFICED YOURSELF TO SAVE THE WORLD.
WE GAVE YOU ***A HERO'S FUNERAL.***
YOU DID...?
THANK YOU.
YOU PILOTED A ROCKET INTO THE HEART OF AN ASTEROID BIG ENOUGH TO DESTROY THIS PLANET.
HOW COULD YOU HAVE POSSIBLY SURVIVED?
I...DON'T KNOW. I MUST'VE ABSORBED A MASSIVE AMOUNT OF RADIATION...
I'M JUST GLAD I MADE IT BACK AND THAT EARTH IS SAFE.
YOU--KEPT REFERRING TO YOURSELF IN THE PLURAL, LIKE *"WE"* AND *"US."* WHAT WAS THAT ABOUT?
I...IT'S LIKE A FOG'S BEEN LIFTED AFTER A VERY LONG TIME.
YOU THREATENED TO KILL US BOTH.
WHY WOULD I DO THAT?
I HATE BREAKING UP THIS LITTLE FUJI MOMENT--
-- BUT AT THIRTEEN YEARS OLD I HOPE I'M NOT ***THE ONLY ONE*** HERE WHO KNOWS THAT ENERGY CAN'T BE ***DESTROYED...***
...IT CAN ONLY BE ***CONVERTED*** FROM ONE FORM TO ANOTHER.
SO, MY QUESTION IS...
...WHAT DO I DO WITH IT ***NOW?***

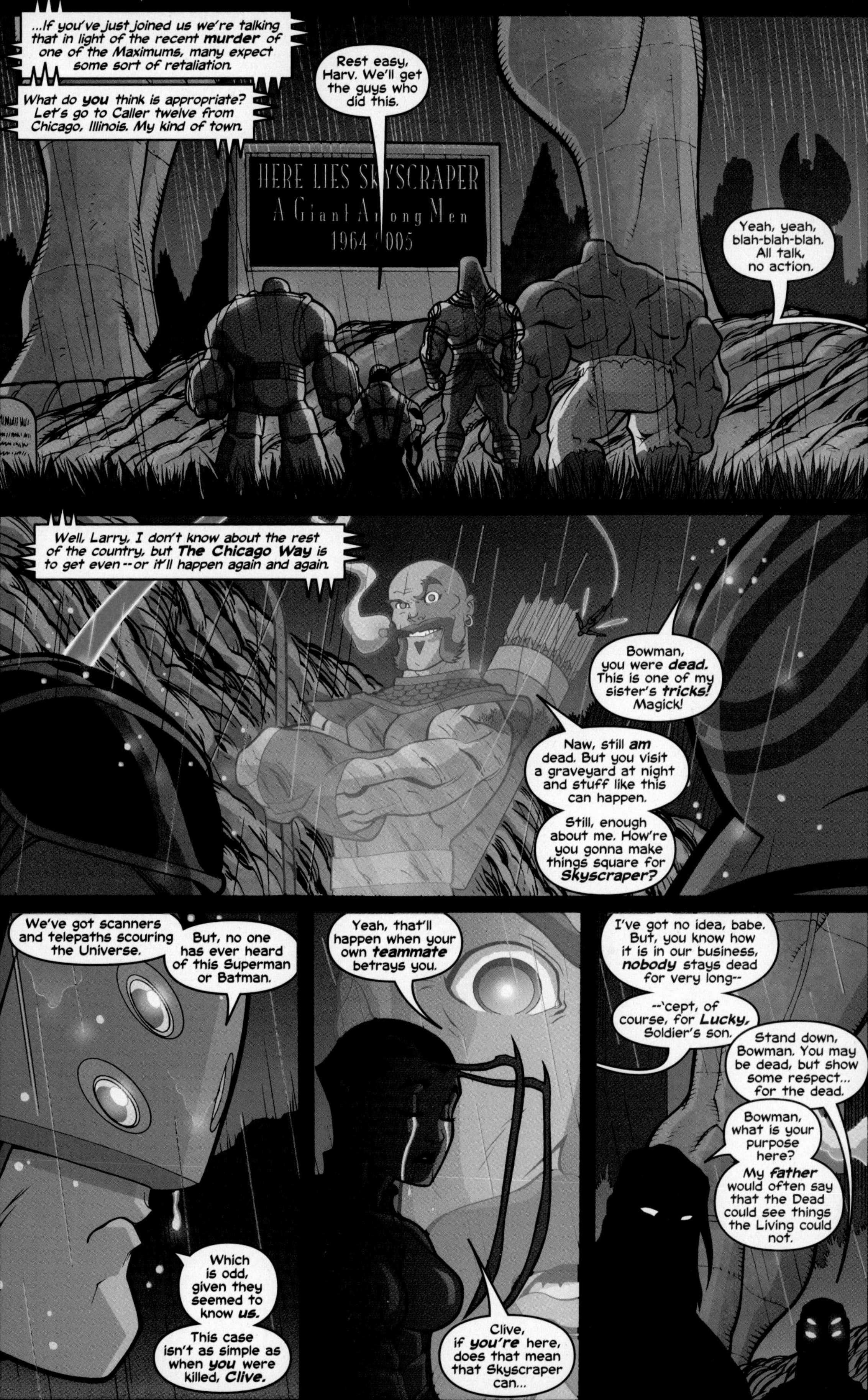
...If you've just joined us we're talking that in light of the recent murder of one of the Maximums, many expect some sort of retaliation.
What do you think is appropriate? Let's go to Caller twelve from Chicago, Illinois. My kind of town.
Rest easy, Harv. We'll get the guys who did this.
HERE LIES SKYSCRAPER
A Giant Among Men
1964-2005
Yeah, yeah, blah-blah-blah. All talk, no action.
Well, Larry, I don't know about the rest of the country, but The Chicago Way is to get even--or it'll happen again and again.
Bowman, you were dead. This is one of my sister's tricks! Magick!
Naw, still am dead. But you visit a graveyard at night and stuff like this can happen.
Still, enough about me. How're you gonna make things square for Skyscraper?
We've got scanners and telepaths scouring the Universe.
But, no one has ever heard of this Superman or Batman.
Which is odd, given they seemed to know us.
This case isn't as simple as when you were killed, Clive.
Yeah, that'll happen when your own teammate betrays you.
Clive, if you're here, does that mean that Skyscraper can...
I've got no idea, babe. But, you know how it is in our business, nobody stays dead for very long--
--'cept, of course, for Lucky, Soldier's son.
Stand down, Bowman. You may be dead, but show some respect... for the dead.
Bowman, what is your purpose here?
My father would often say that the Dead could see things the Living could not.

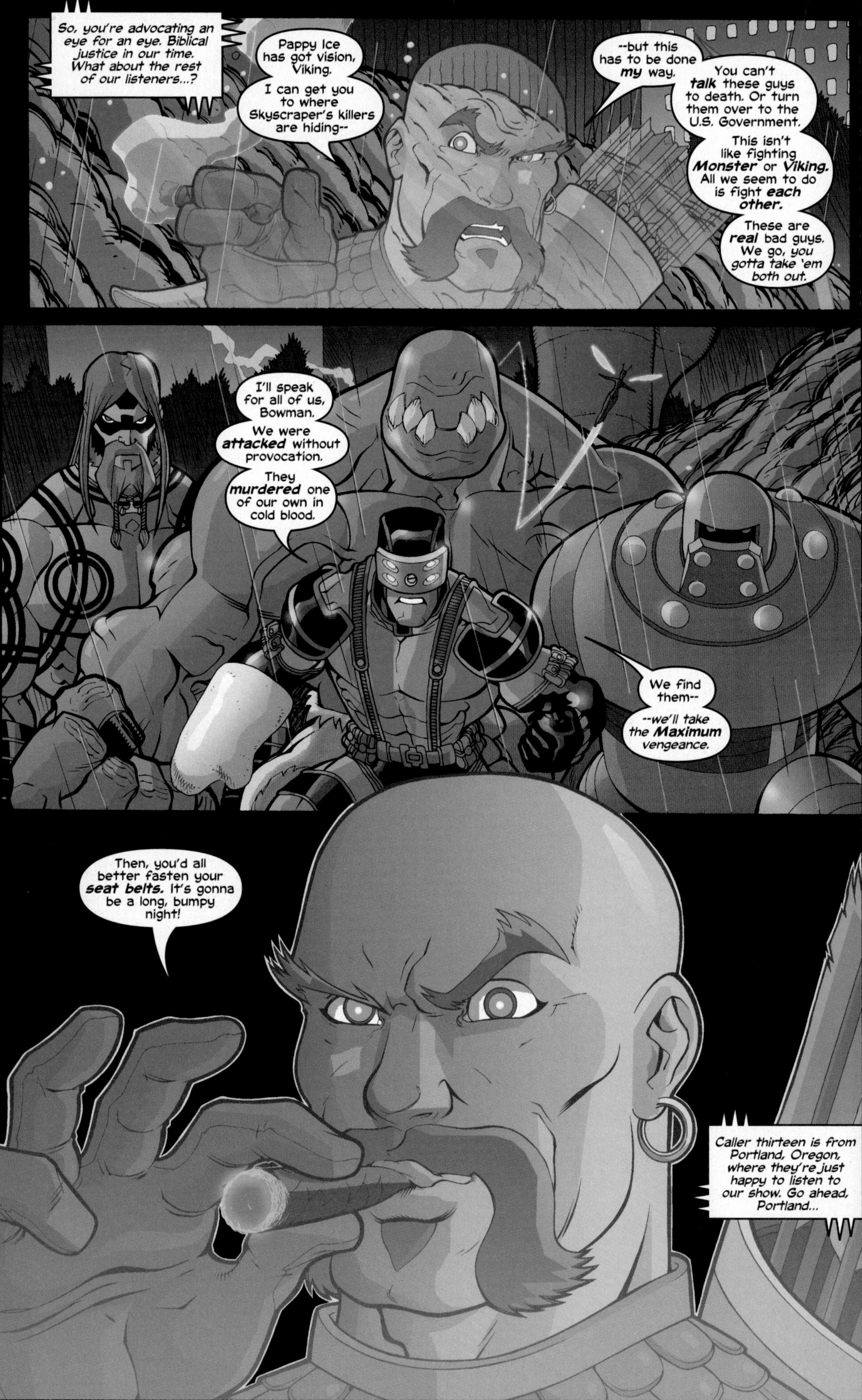
So, you're advocating an eye for an eye. Biblical justice in our time. What about the rest of our listeners...?
Pappy Ice has got vision, Viking.
I can get you to where Skyscraper's killers are hiding--
--but this has to be done my way.
You can't talk these guys to death. Or turn them over to the U.S. Government.
This isn't like fighting Monster or Viking. All we seem to do is fight each other.
These are real bad guys. We go, you gotta take 'em both out.
I'll speak for all of us, Bowman.
We were attacked without provocation.
They murdered one of our own in cold blood.
We find them--
--we'll take the Maximum vengeance.
Then, you'd all better fasten your seat belts. It's gonna be a long, bumpy night!
Caller thirteen is from Portland, Oregon, where they're just happy to listen to our show. Go ahead, Portland...

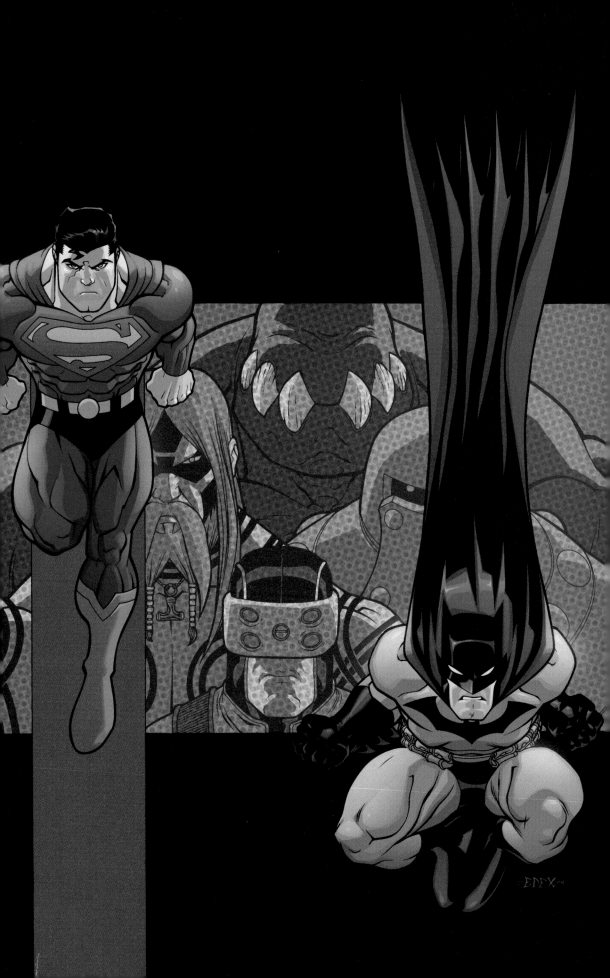

"MISTAKEN IDENTITY CRISIS"

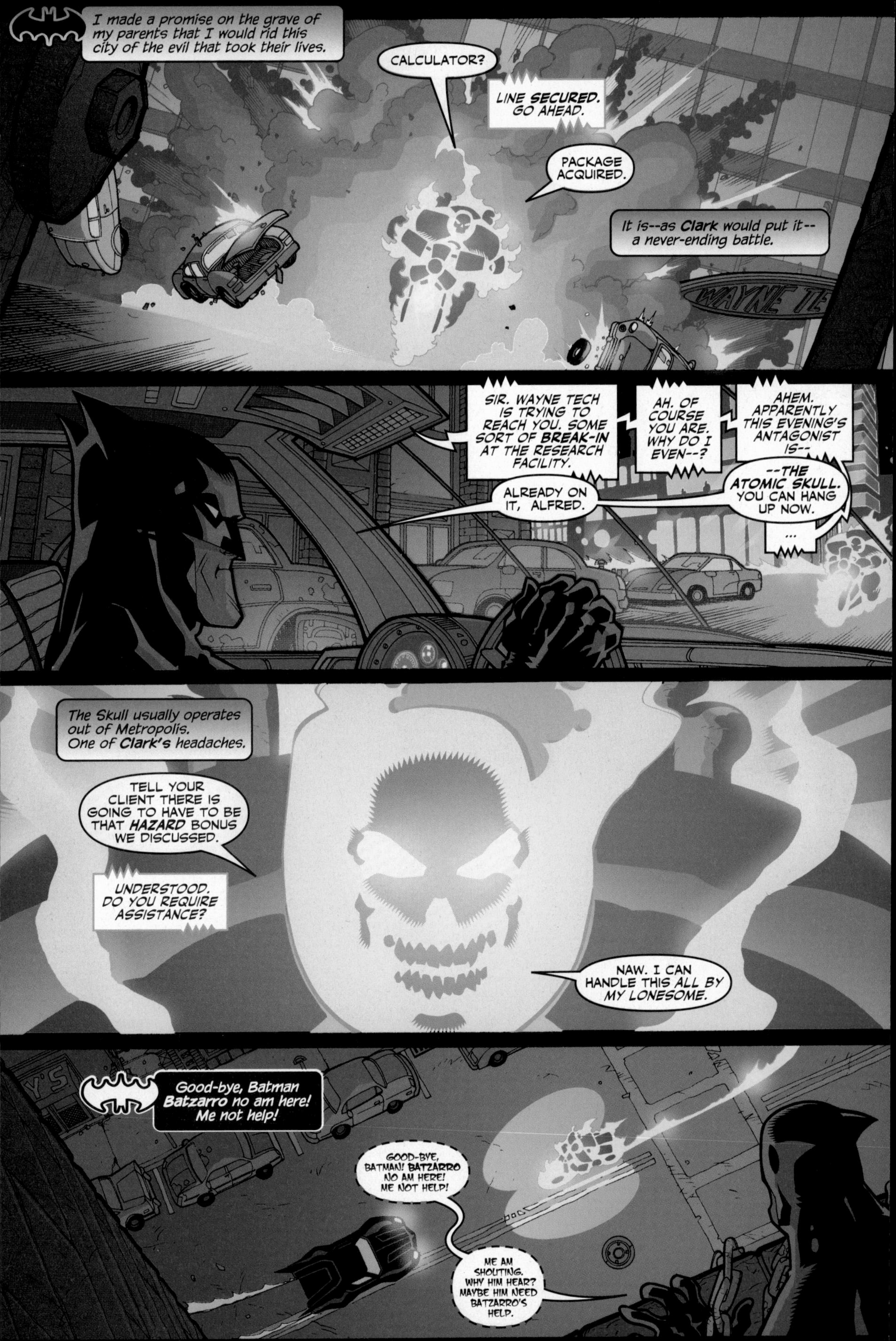
I made a promise on the grave of my parents that I would rid this city of the evil that took their lives.
CALCULATOR?
LINE SECURED. GO AHEAD.
PACKAGE ACQUIRED.
It is--as Clark would put it--a never-ending battle.
WAYNE TE
SIR. WAYNE TECH IS TRYING TO REACH YOU. SOME SORT OF BREAK-IN AT THE RESEARCH FACILITY.
AH. OF COURSE YOU ARE. WHY DO I EVEN--?
AHEM. APPARENTLY THIS EVENING'S ANTAGONIST IS--
ALREADY ON IT, ALFRED.
--THE ATOMIC SKULL. YOU CAN HANG UP NOW.
...
The Skull usually operates out of Metropolis. One of Clark's headaches.
TELL YOUR CLIENT THERE IS GOING TO HAVE TO BE THAT HAZARD BONUS WE DISCUSSED.
UNDERSTOOD. DO YOU REQUIRE ASSISTANCE?
NAW. I CAN HANDLE THIS ALL BY MY LONESOME.
Good-bye, Batman Batzarro no am here! Me not help!
GOOD-BYE, BATMAN! BATZARRO NO AM HERE! ME NOT HELP!
ME AM SHOUTING. WHY HIM HEAR? MAYBE HIM NEED BATZARRO'S HELP.

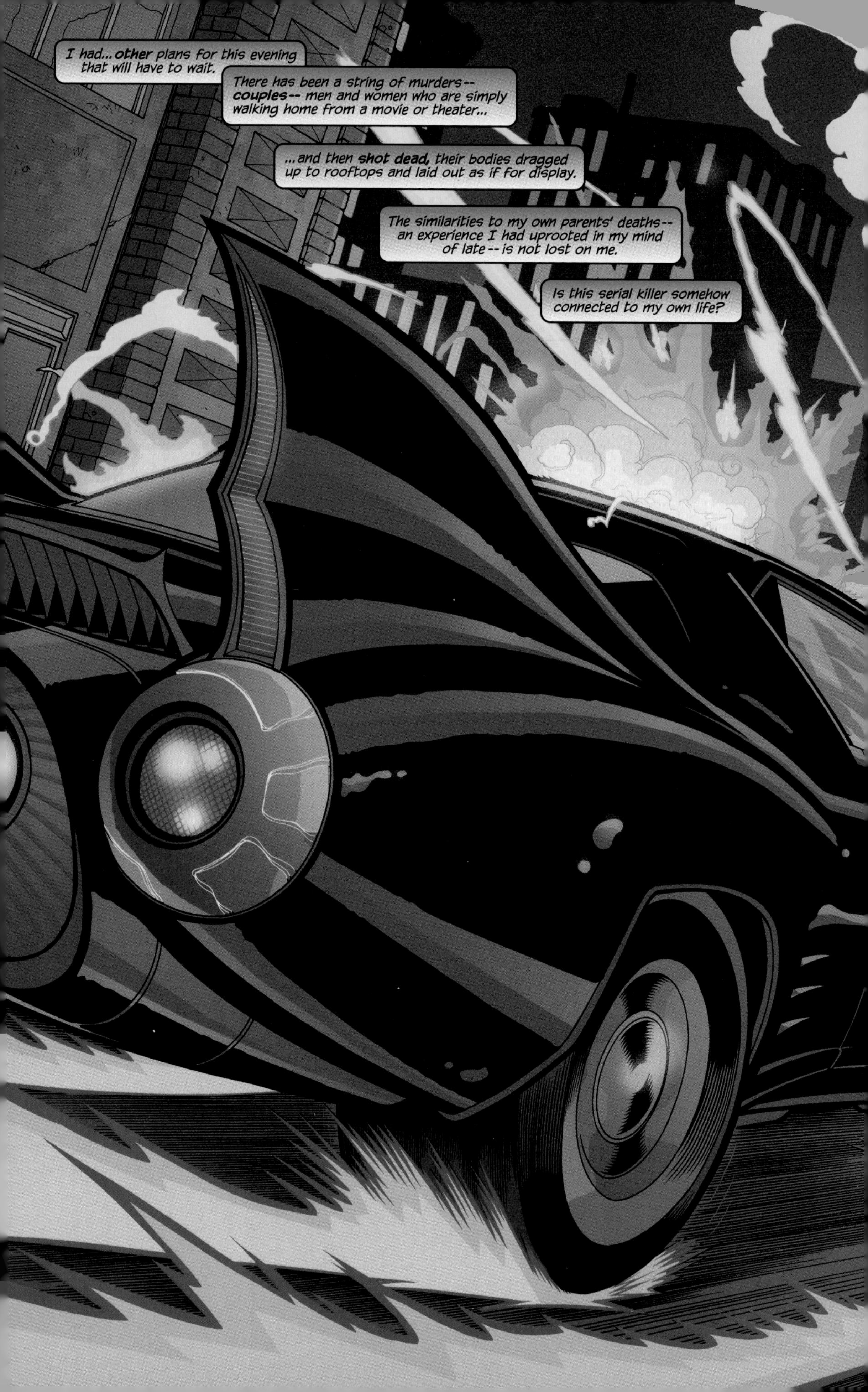
I had... **other** plans for this evening that will have to wait.
There has been a string of murders-- **couples--** men and women who are simply walking home from a movie or theater...
...and then **shot dead,** their bodies dragged up to rooftops and laid out as if for display.
The similarities to my own parents' deaths-- an experience I had uprooted in my mind of late-- is not lost on me.
Is this serial killer somehow connected to my own life?

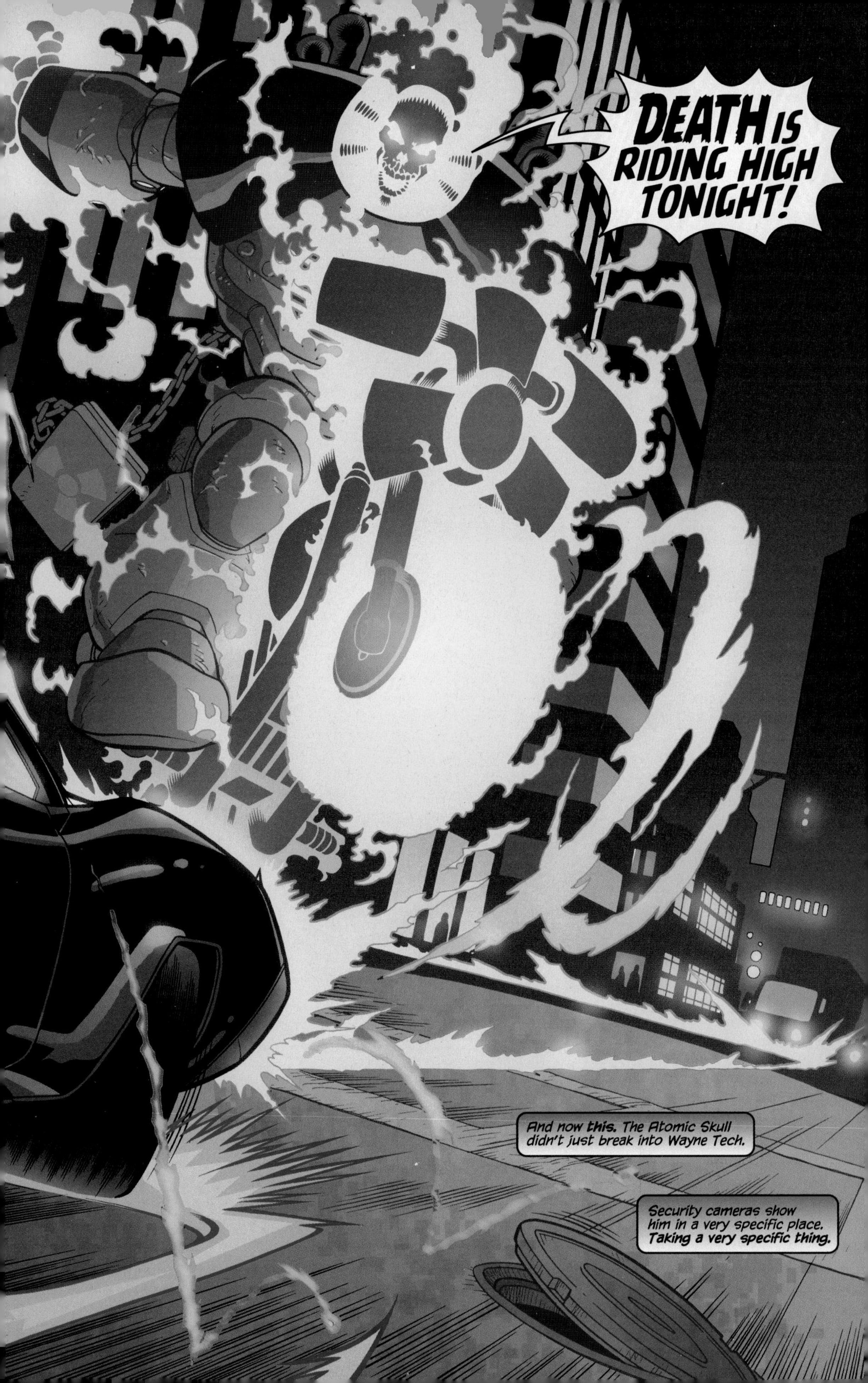
DEATH IS RIDING HIGH TONIGHT!
And now this. The Atomic Skull didn't just break into Wayne Tech.
Security cameras show him in a very specific place. Taking a very specific thing.

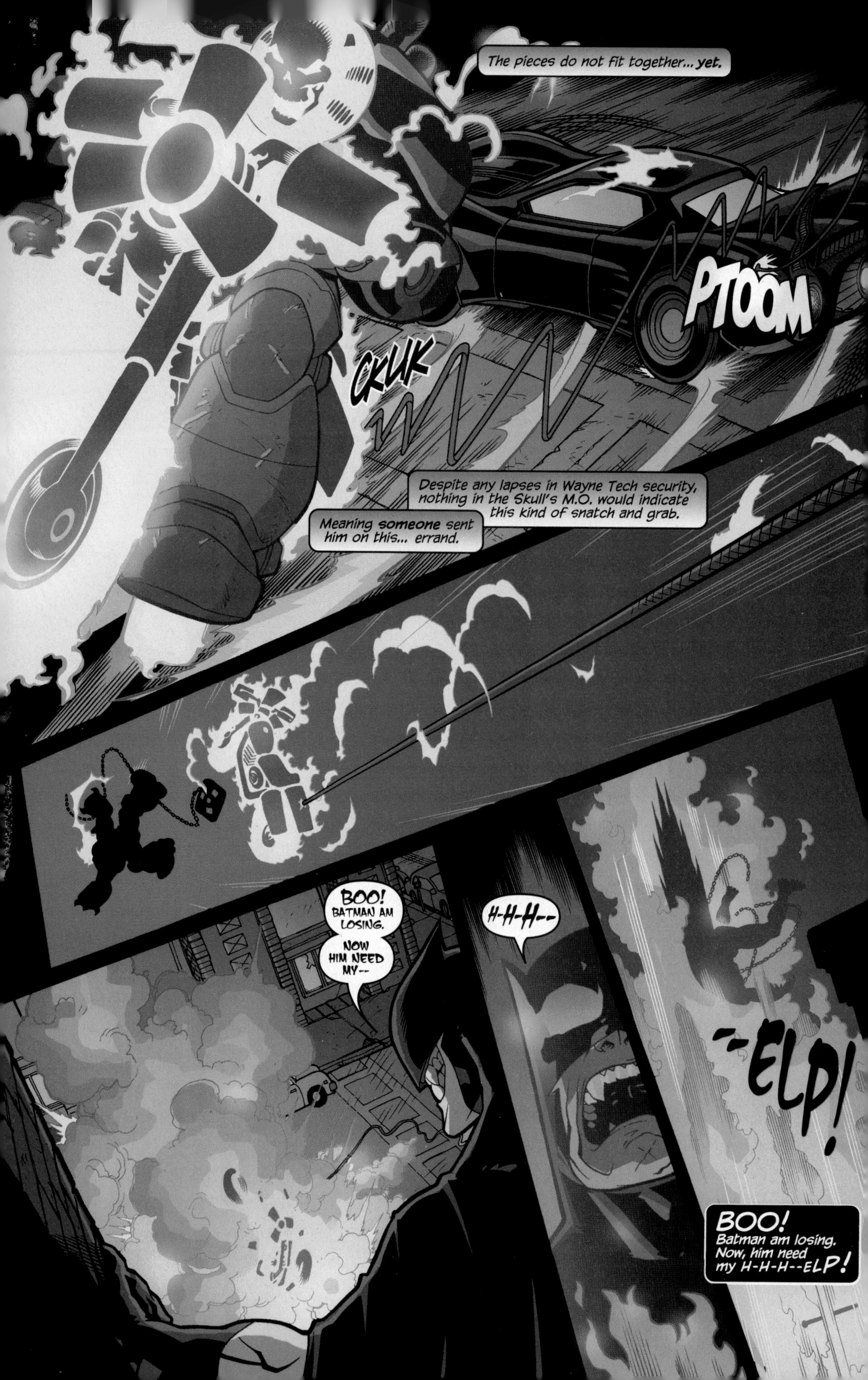

The pieces do not fit together... **yet.**
PTOOM
CKUK
Despite any lapses in Wayne Tech security, nothing in the Skull's M.O. would indicate this kind of snatch and grab.
Meaning **someone** sent him on this... errand.
BOO! BATMAN AM LOSING.
NOW HIM NEED MY--
H-H-H--
--ELP!
BOO!
Batman am losing.
Now, him need my H-H-H--ELP!

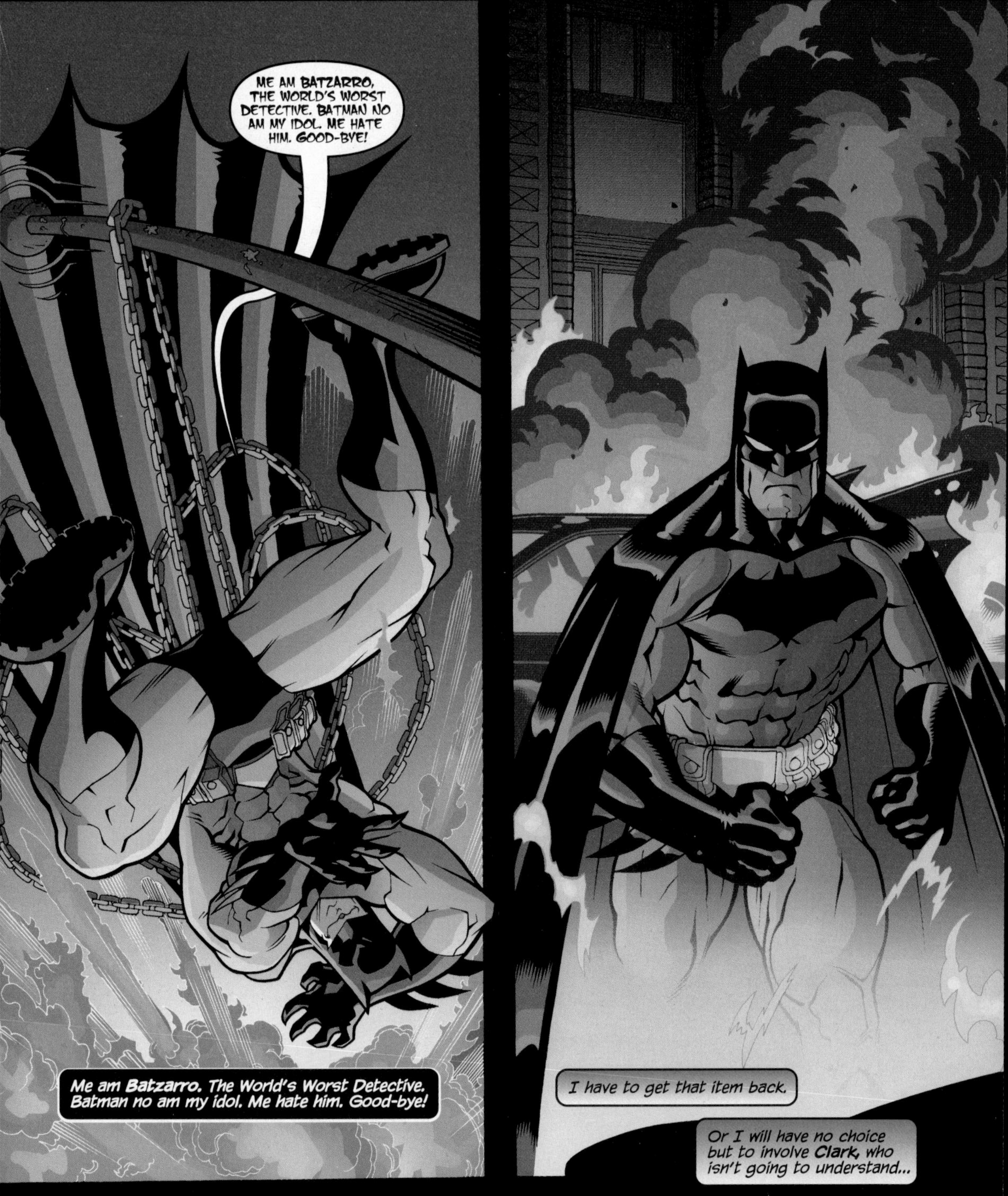
ME AM BATZARRO, THE WORLD'S WORST DETECTIVE. BATMAN NO AM MY IDOL. ME HATE HIM. GOOD-BYE!
Me am Batzarro. The World's Worst Detective. Batman no am my idol. Me hate him. Good-bye!
I have to get that item back.
Or I will have no choice but to involve Clark, who isn't going to understand...

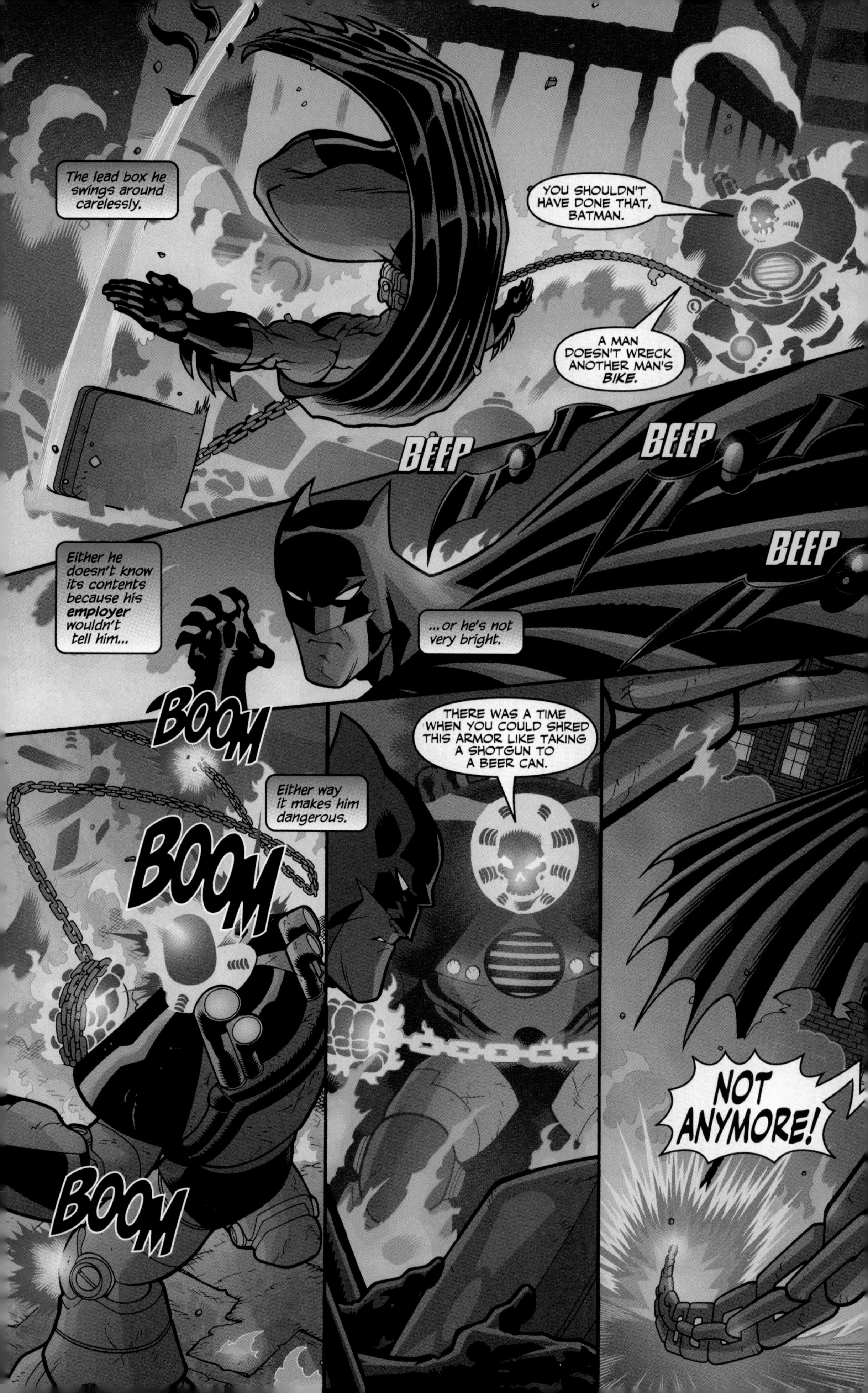
The lead box he swings around carelessly.
YOU SHOULDN'T HAVE DONE THAT, BATMAN.
A MAN DOESN'T WRECK ANOTHER MAN'S BIKE.
BEEP
BEEP
BEEP
Either he doesn't know its contents because his employer wouldn't tell him...
...or he's not very bright.
BOOM
BOOM
BOOM
Either way it makes him dangerous.
THERE WAS A TIME WHEN YOU COULD SHRED THIS ARMOR LIKE TAKING A SHOTGUN TO A BEER CAN.
NOT ANYMORE!

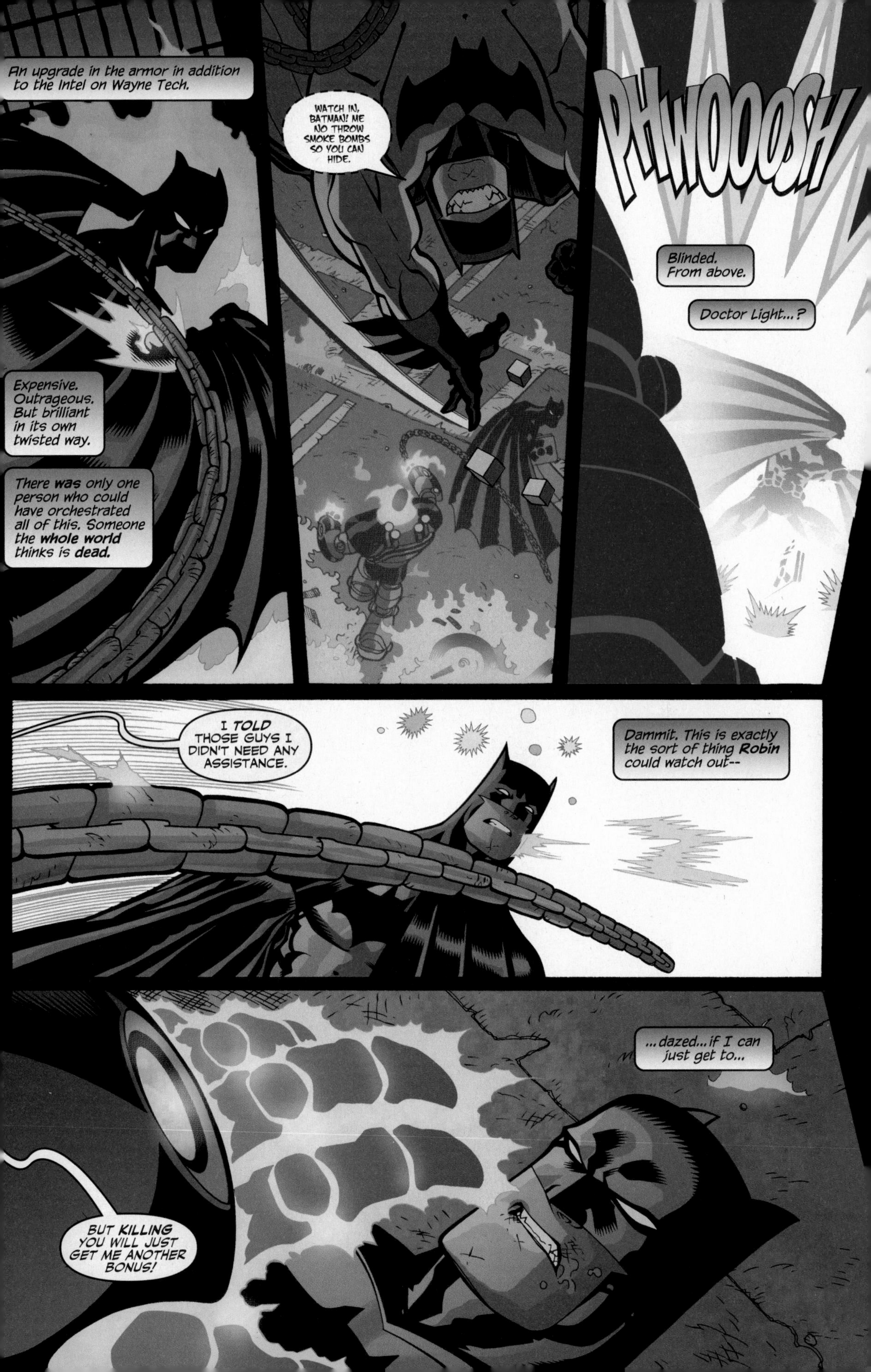
An upgrade in the armor in addition to the Intel on Wayne Tech.
Expensive. Outrageous. But brilliant in its own twisted way.
There was only one person who could have orchestrated all of this. Someone the whole world thinks is dead.
WATCH IN, BATMAN! ME NO THROW SMOKE BOMBS SO YOU CAN HIDE.
PHWOOOSH
Blinded. From above.
Doctor Light...?
I TOLD THOSE GUYS I DIDN'T NEED ANY ASSISTANCE.
Dammit. This is exactly the sort of thing Robin could watch out--
...dazed...if I can just get to...
BUT KILLING YOU WILL JUST GET ME ANOTHER BONUS!

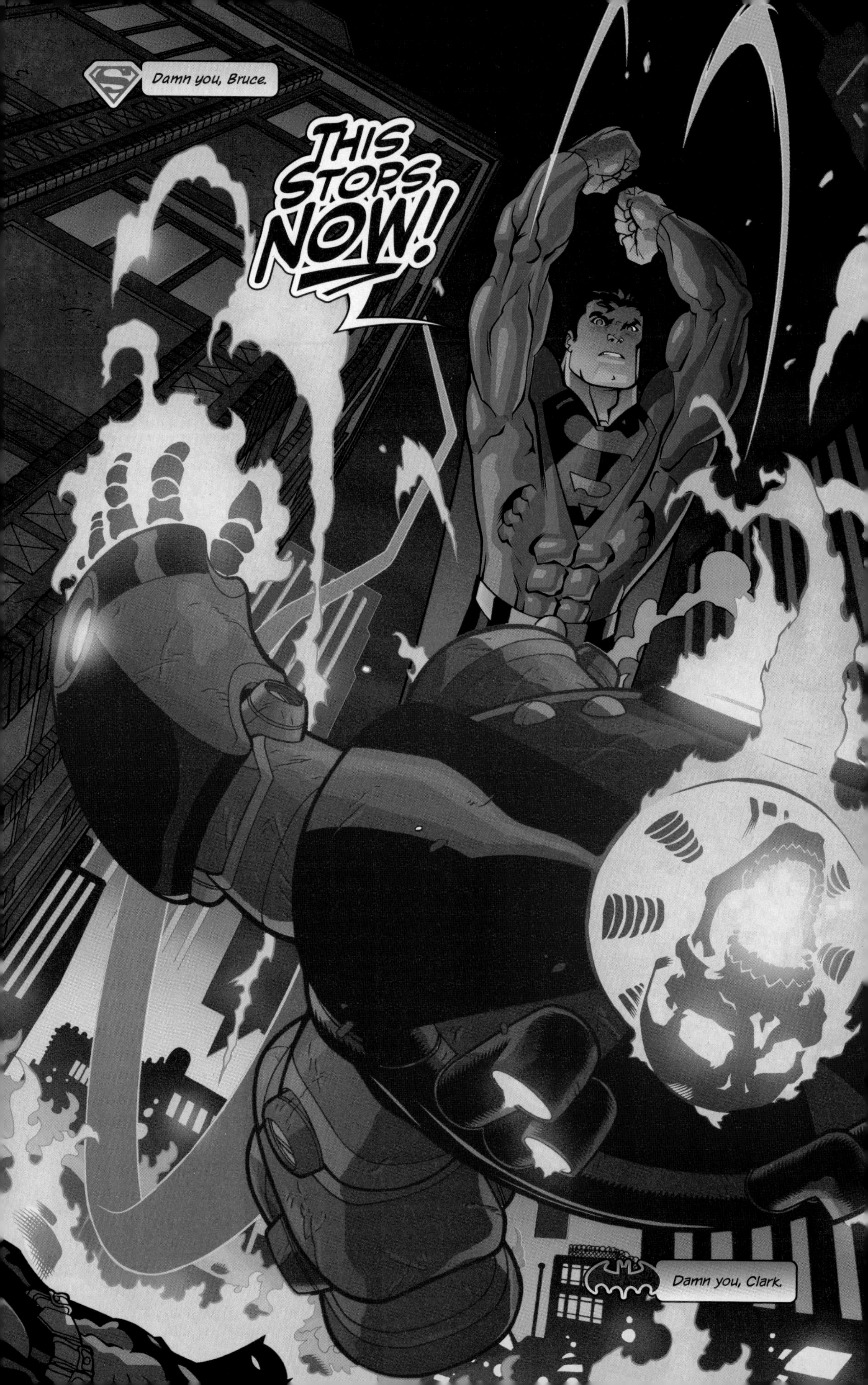
Damn you, Bruce.
THIS STOPS NOW!
Damn you, Clark.

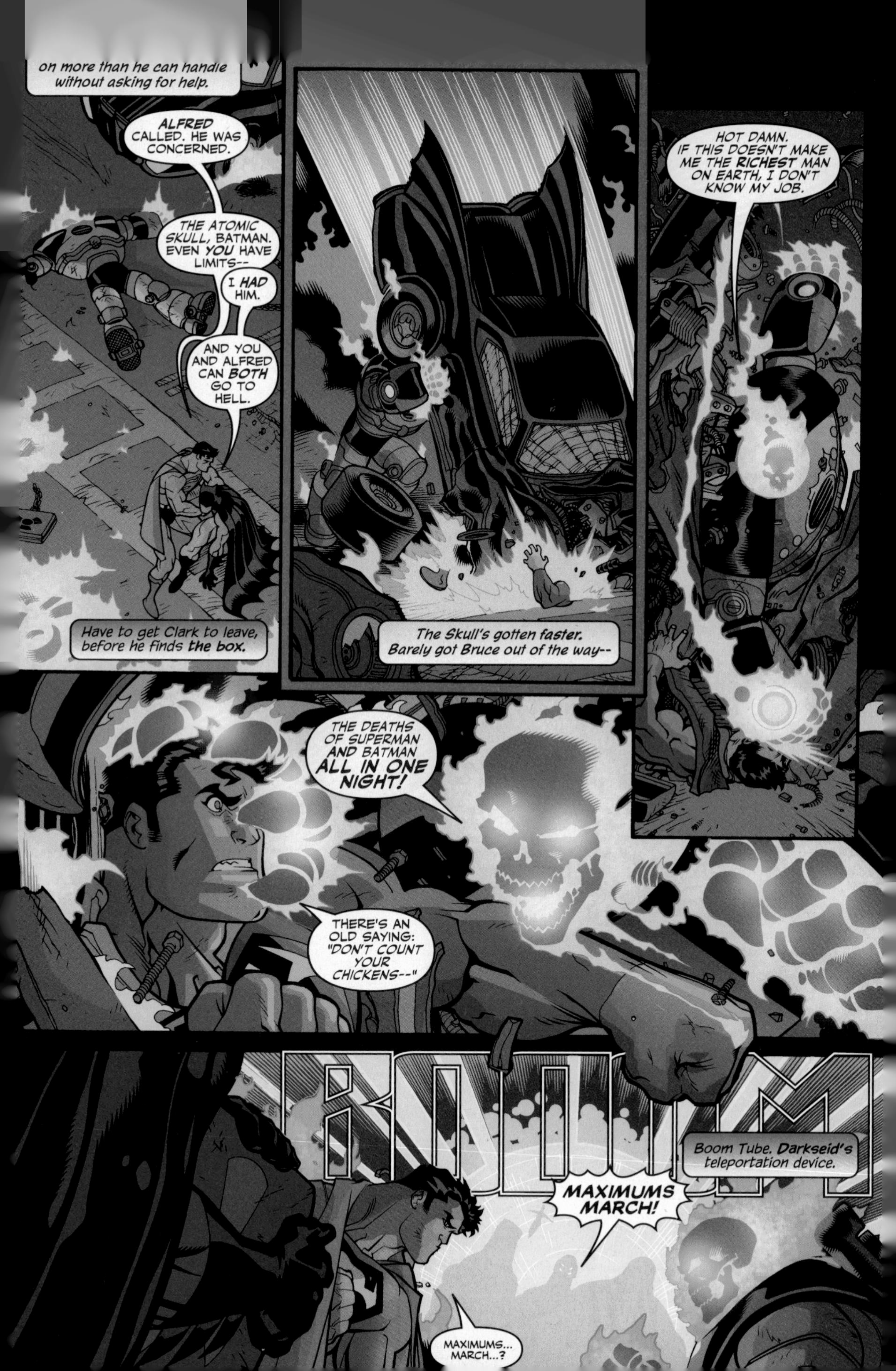
on more than he can handle without asking for help.
ALFRED CALLED. HE WAS CONCERNED.
THE ATOMIC SKULL, BATMAN. EVEN YOU HAVE LIMITS--
I HAD HIM.
AND YOU AND ALFRED CAN BOTH GO TO HELL.
Have to get Clark to leave, before he finds the box.
The Skull's gotten faster. Barely got Bruce out of the way--
HOT DAMN. IF THIS DOESN'T MAKE ME THE RICHEST MAN ON EARTH, I DON'T KNOW MY JOB.
THE DEATHS OF SUPERMAN AND BATMAN ALL IN ONE NIGHT!
THERE'S AN OLD SAYING: "DON'T COUNT YOUR CHICKENS--"
BOOM
Boom Tube. Darkseid's teleportation device.
MAXIMUMS MARCH!
MAXIMUMS... MARCH...?

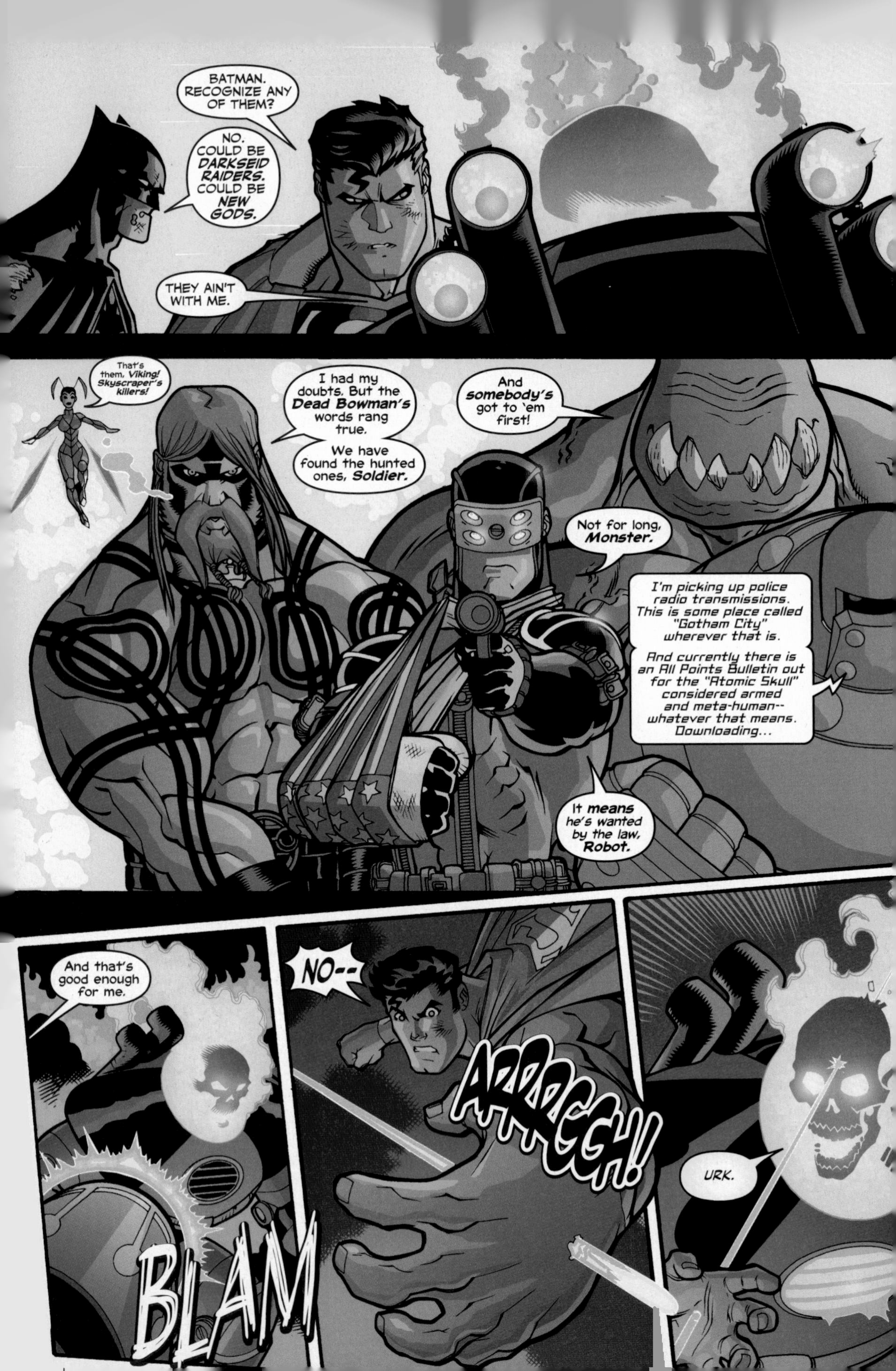
BATMAN. RECOGNIZE ANY OF THEM?
NO. COULD BE DARKSEID RAIDERS. COULD BE NEW GODS.
THEY AIN'T WITH ME.
That's them, Viking! Skyscraper's killers!
I had my doubts. But the Dead Bowman's words rang true.
We have found the hunted ones, Soldier.
And somebody's got to 'em first!
Not for long, Monster.
I'm picking up police radio transmissions. This is some place called "Gotham City" wherever that is.
And currently there is an All Points Bulletin out for the "Atomic Skull" considered armed and meta-human--whatever that means. Downloading...
It means he's wanted by the law, Robot.
And that's good enough for me.
NO--
BLAM
ARRRGGH!
URK.

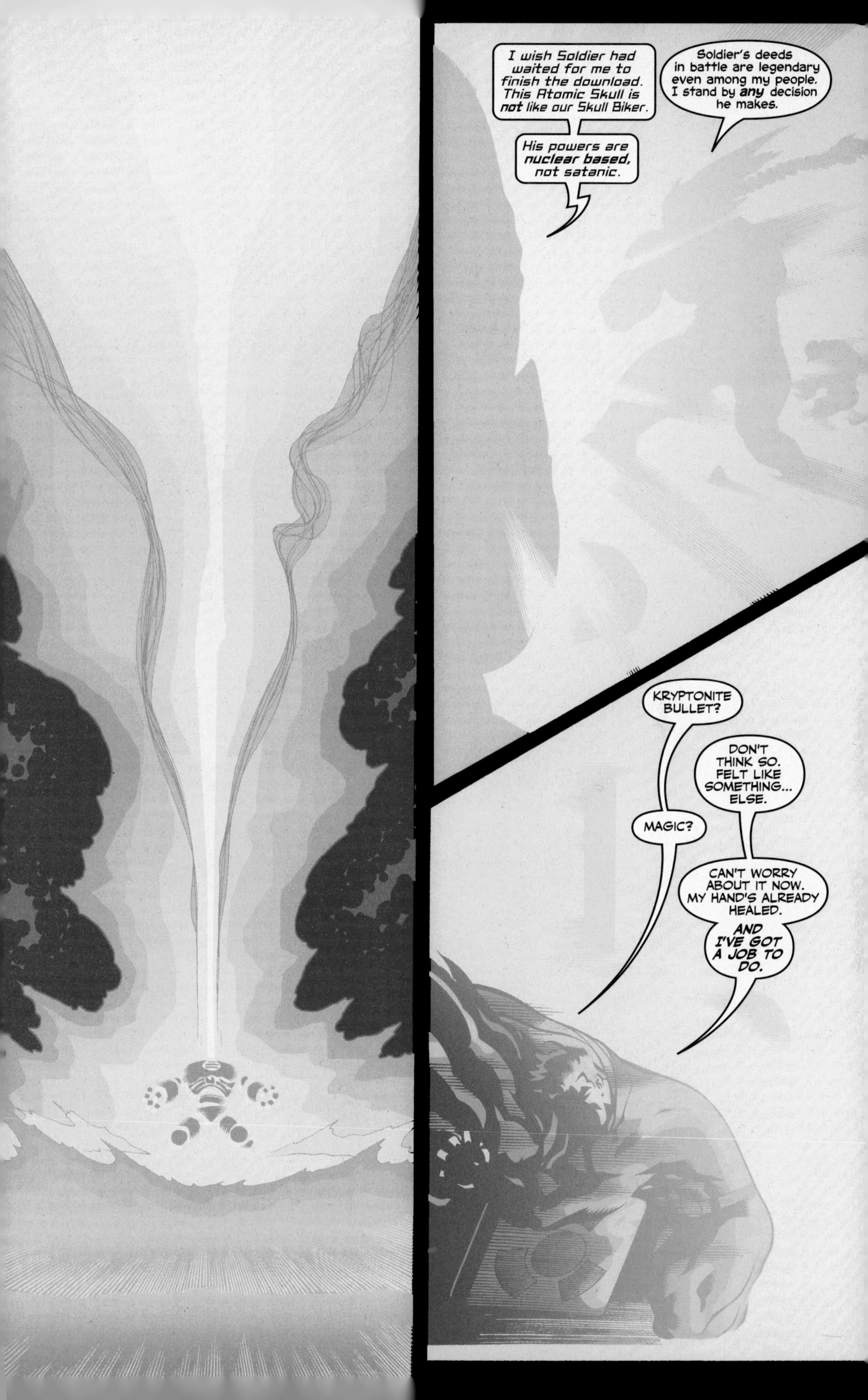
I wish Soldier had waited for me to finish the download. This Atomic Skull is *not* like our Skull Biker.
His powers are *nuclear based,* not satanic.
Soldier's deeds in battle are legendary even among my people. I stand by *any* decision he makes.
KRYPTONITE BULLET?
DON'T THINK SO. FELT LIKE SOMETHING... ELSE.
MAGIC?
CAN'T WORRY ABOUT IT NOW. MY HAND'S ALREADY HEALED.
AND I'VE GOT A JOB TO DO.

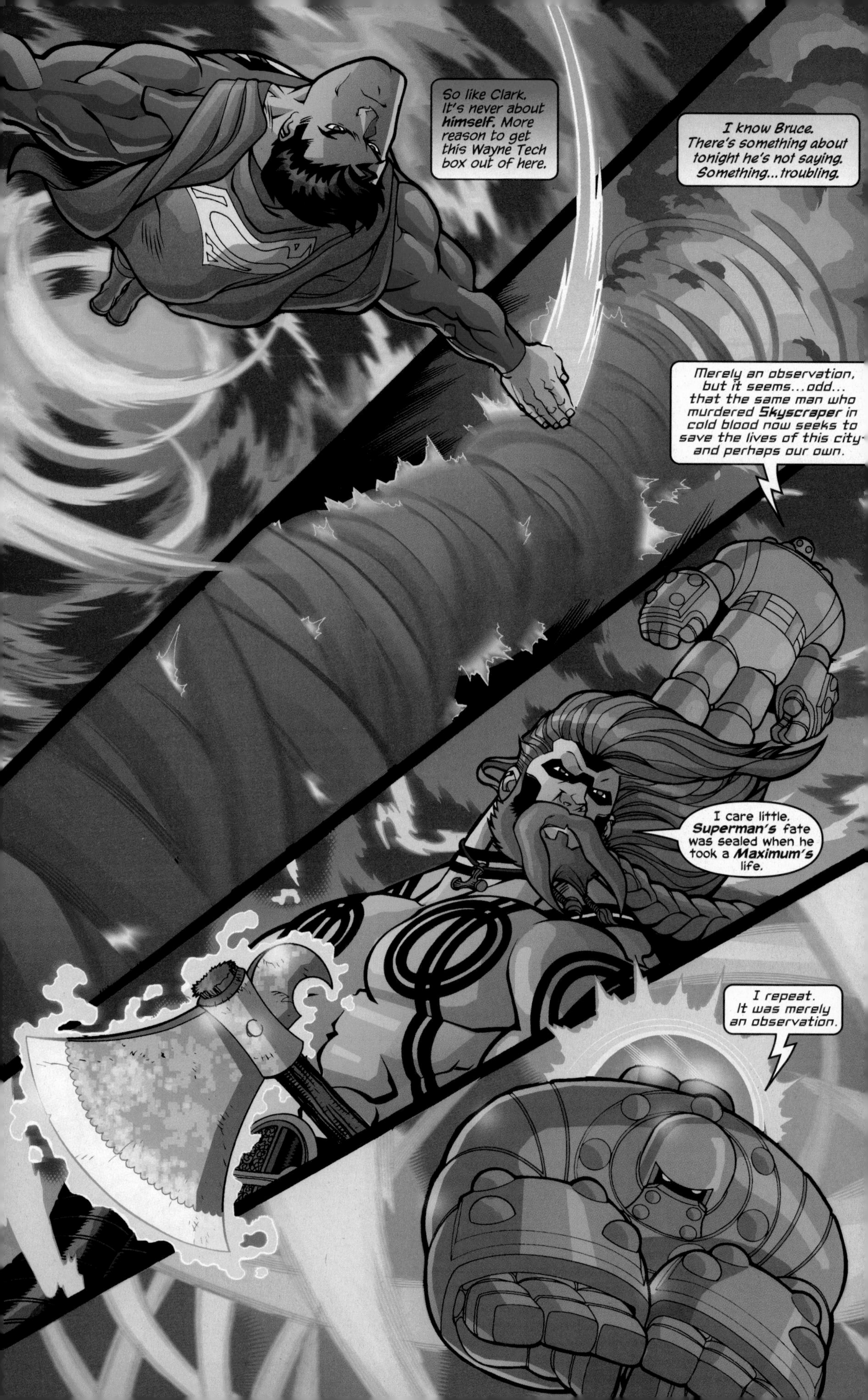
So like Clark. It's never about **himself.** More reason to get this Wayne Tech box out of here.
I know Bruce. There's something about tonight he's not saying. Something...troubling.
Merely an observation, but it seems...odd... that the same man who murdered **Skyscraper** in cold blood now seeks to save the lives of this city-and perhaps our own.
I care little. **Superman's** fate was sealed when he took a **Maximum's** life.
I repeat. It was merely an observation.

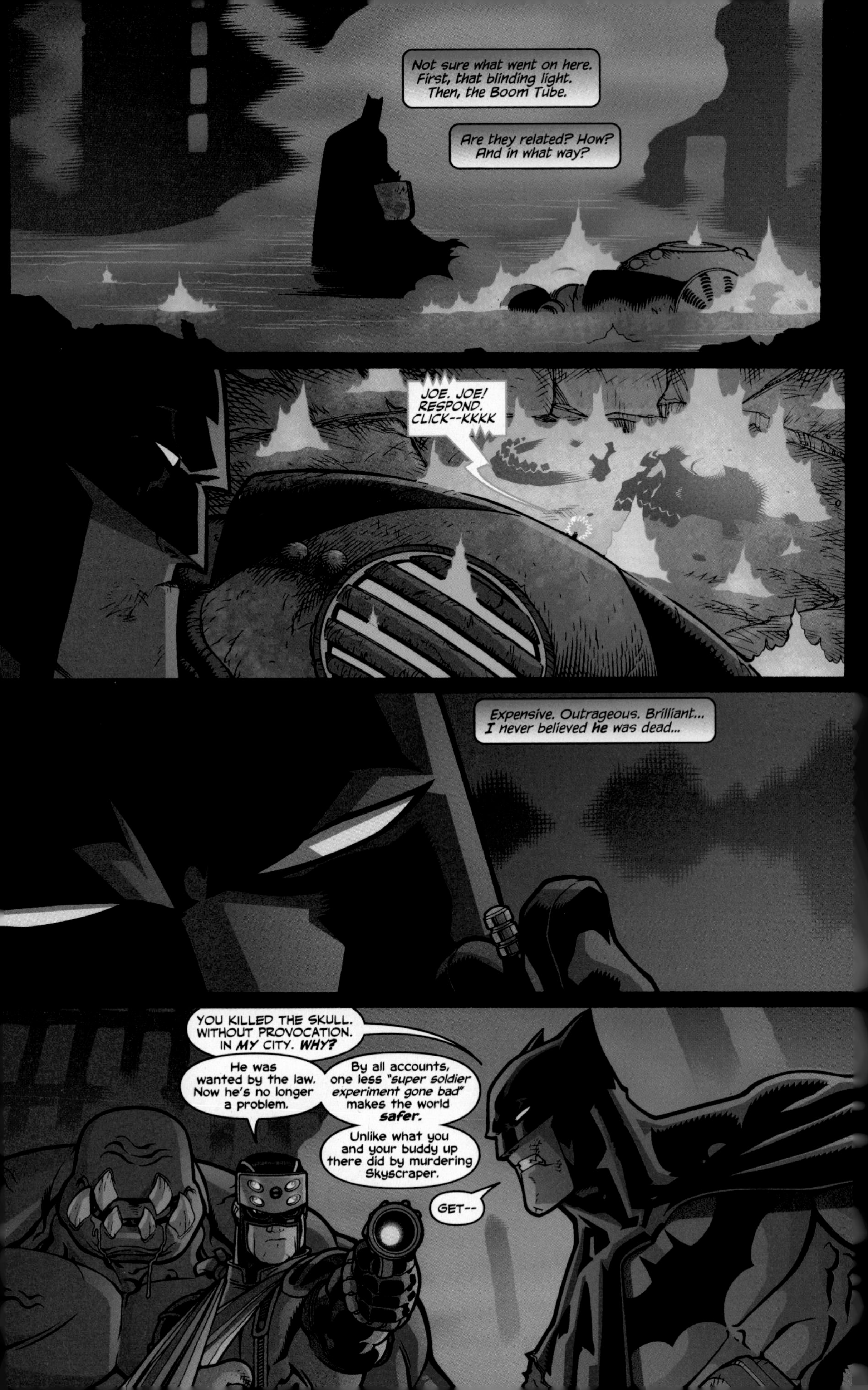

Not sure what went on here. First, that blinding light. Then, the Boom Tube.
Are they related? How? And in what way?
JOE. JOE! RESPOND. CLICK--KKKK
Expensive. Outrageous. Brilliant... I never believed he was dead...
YOU KILLED THE SKULL. WITHOUT PROVOCATION. IN MY CITY. WHY?
He was wanted by the law. Now he's no longer a problem.
By all accounts, one less "super soldier experiment gone bad" makes the world safer.
Unlike what you and your buddy up there did by murdering Skyscraper.
GET--

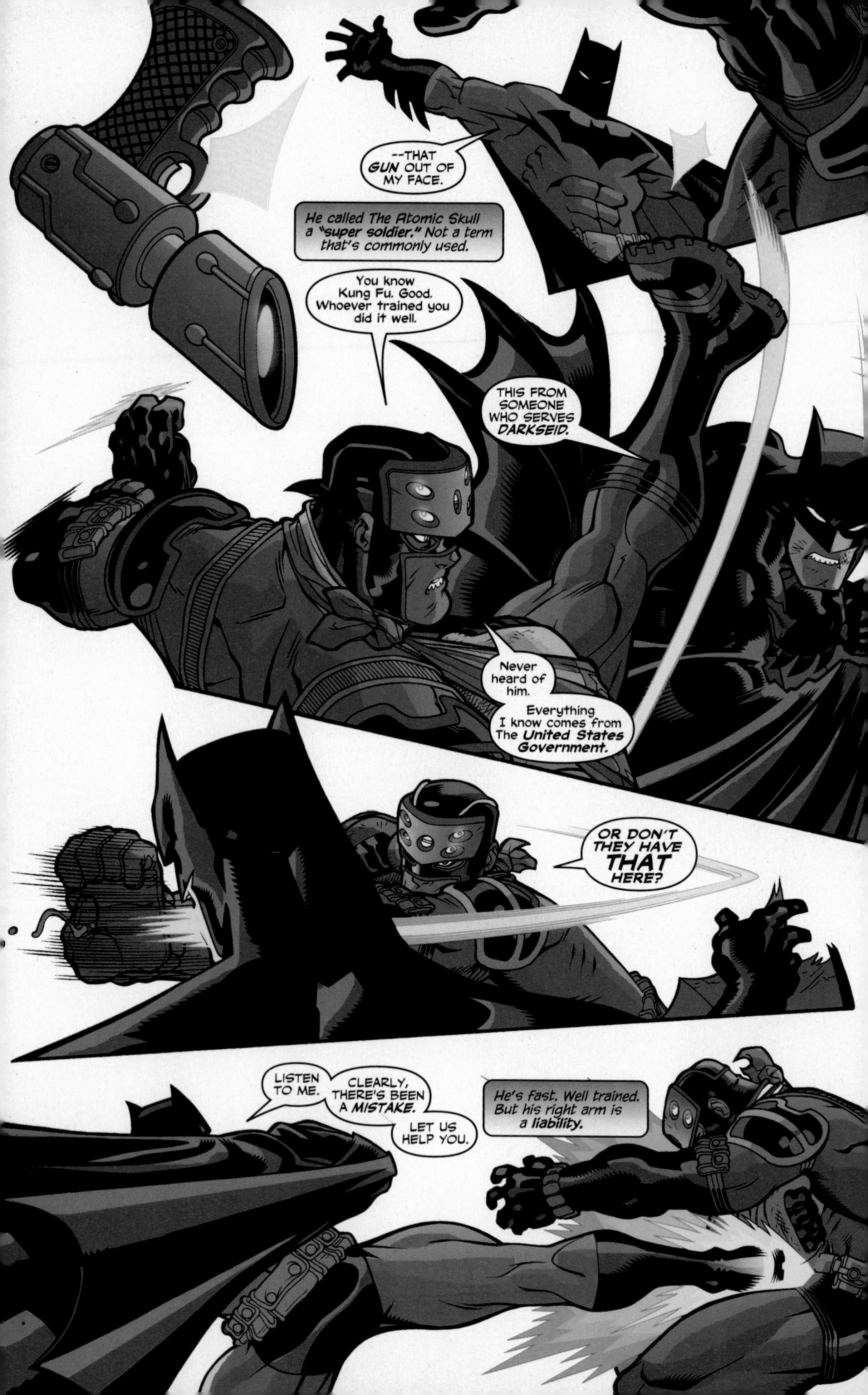

--THAT GUN OUT OF MY FACE.
He called The Atomic Skull a "super soldier." Not a term that's commonly used.
You know Kung Fu. Good. Whoever trained you did it well.
THIS FROM SOMEONE WHO SERVES DARKSEID.
Never heard of him.
Everything I know comes from The United States Government.
OR DON'T THEY HAVE THAT HERE?
LISTEN TO ME.
CLEARLY, THERE'S BEEN A MISTAKE.
LET US HELP YOU.
He's fast. Well trained. But his right arm is a liability.

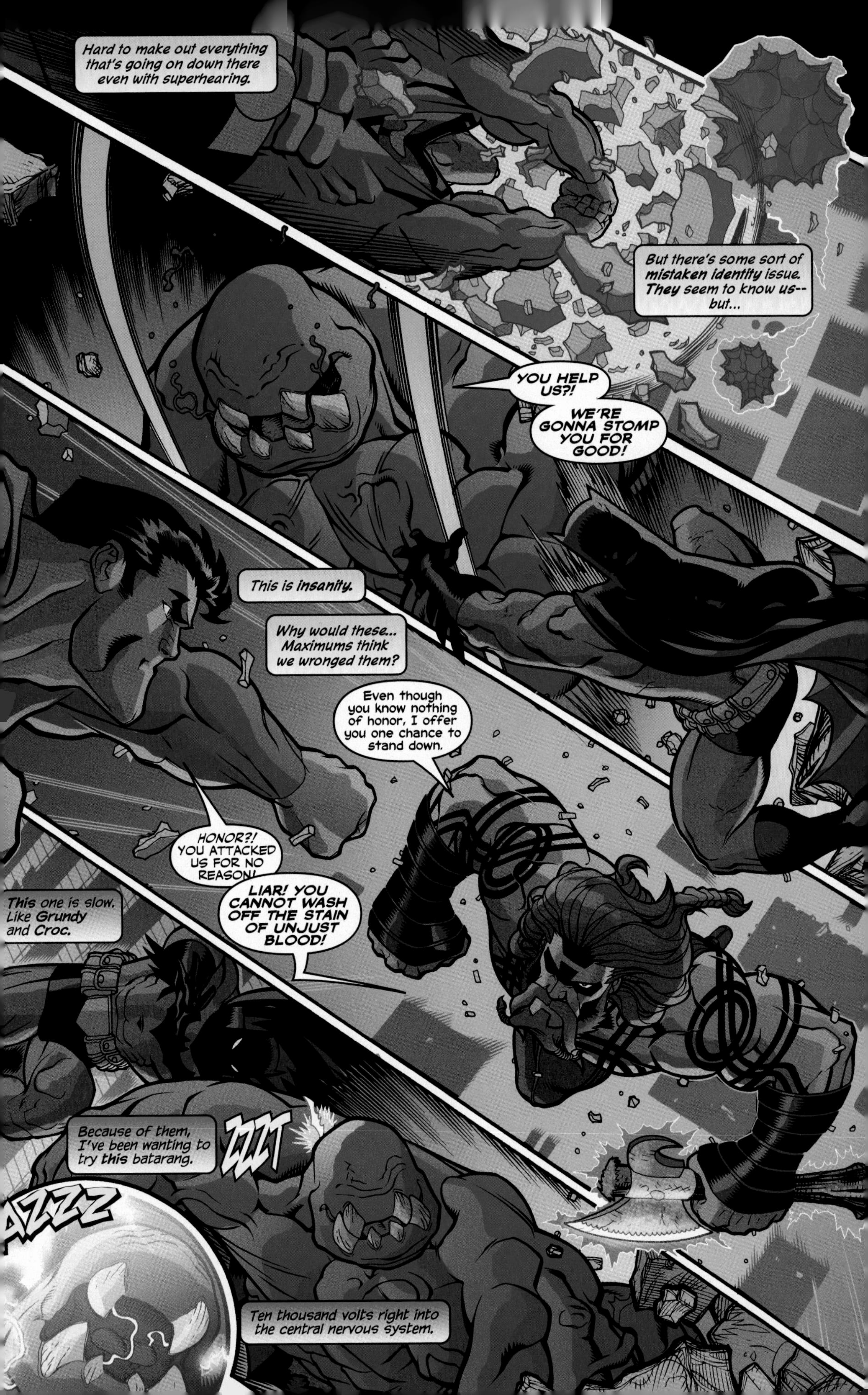
Hard to make out everything that's going on down there even with superhearing.
But there's some sort of mistaken identity issue. They seem to know us-- but...
YOU HELP US?!
WE'RE GONNA STOMP YOU FOR GOOD!
This is insanity.
Why would these... Maximums think we wronged them?
Even though you know nothing of honor, I offer you one chance to stand down.
HONOR?! YOU ATTACKED US FOR NO REASON!
LIAR! YOU CANNOT WASH OFF THE STAIN OF UNJUST BLOOD!
This one is slow. Like Grundy and Croc.
Because of them, I've been wanting to try this batarang.
ZZZT
AZZZZ
Ten thousand volts right into the central nervous system.

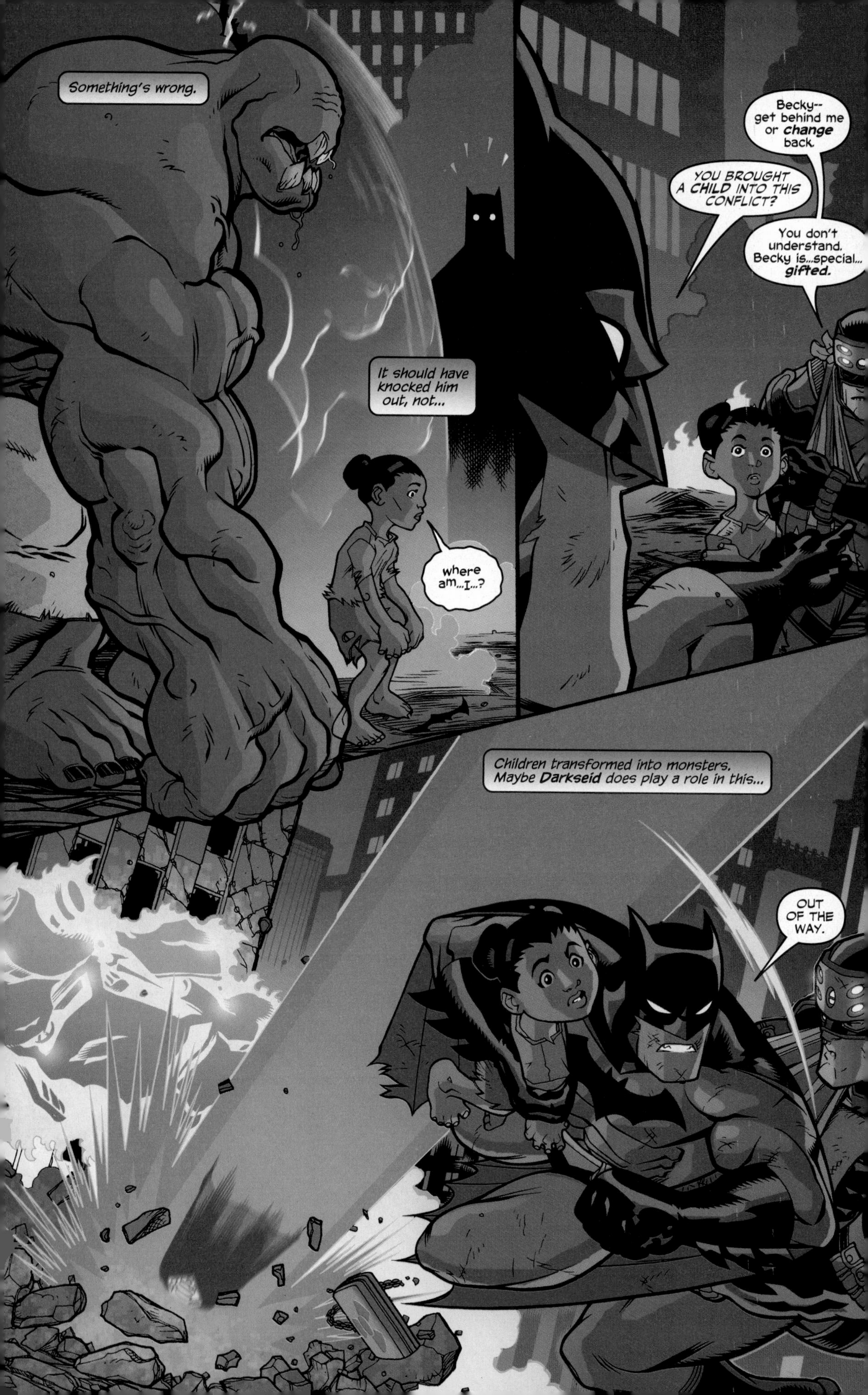
Something's wrong.
It should have knocked him out, not...
where am...I...?
Becky-- get behind me or change back.
YOU BROUGHT A CHILD INTO THIS CONFLICT?
You don't understand. Becky is...special... gifted.
Children transformed into monsters. Maybe Darkseid does play a role in this...
OUT OF THE WAY.

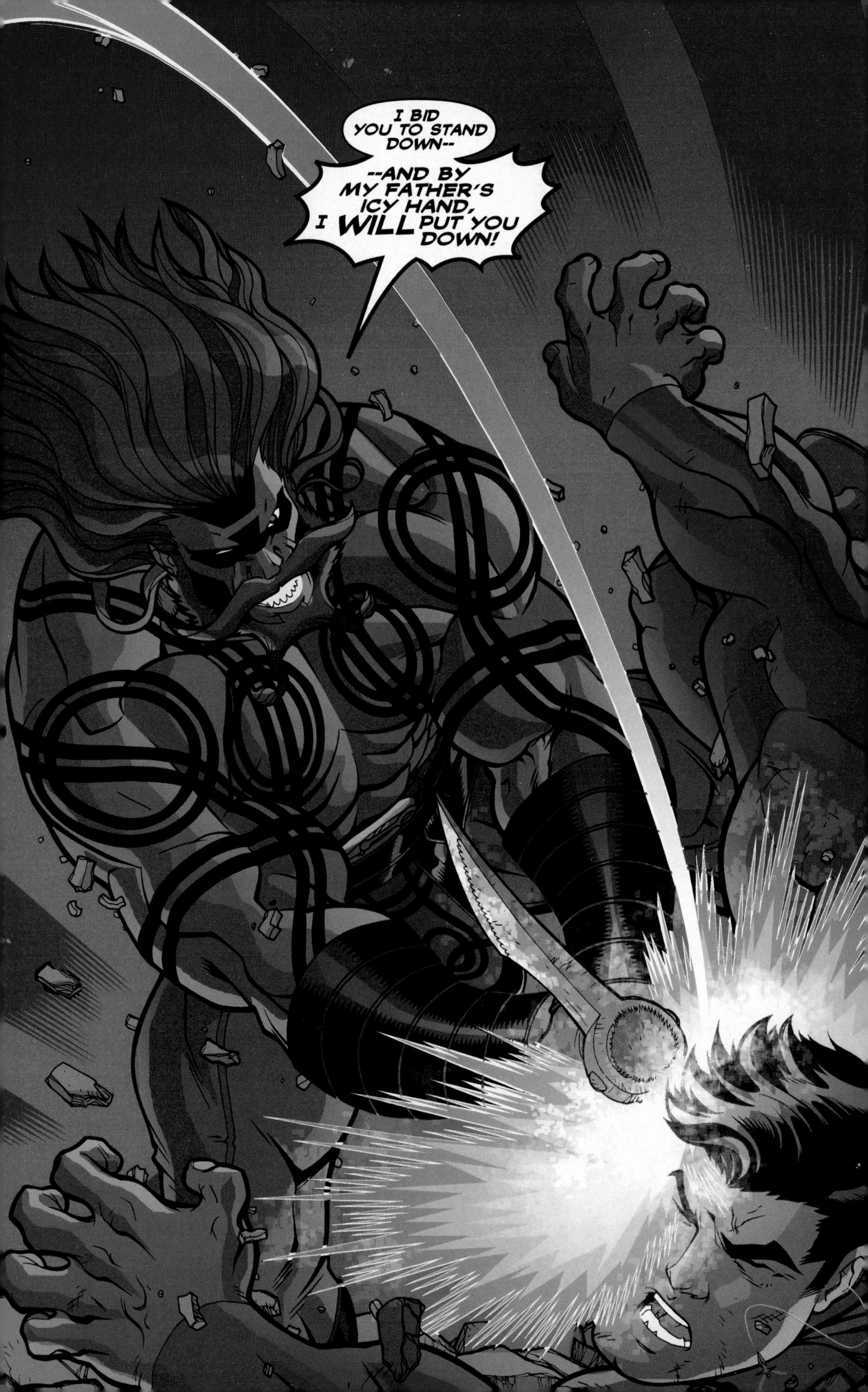
I BID YOU TO STAND DOWN--
--AND BY MY FATHER'S ICY HAND, I WILL PUT YOU DOWN!

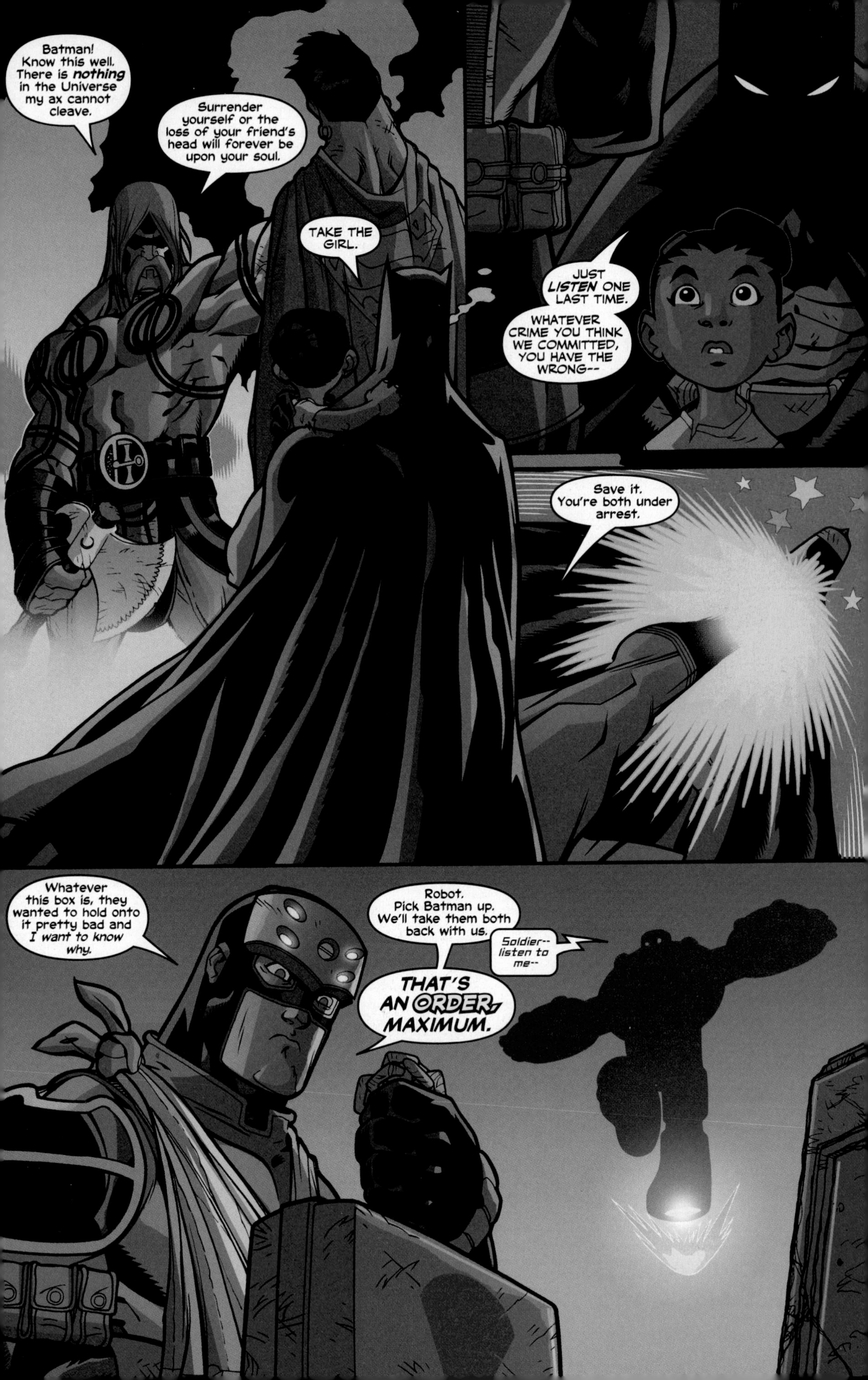
Batman! Know this well. There is *nothing* in the Universe my ax cannot cleave.
Surrender yourself or the loss of your friend's head will forever be upon your soul.
TAKE THE GIRL.
JUST *LISTEN* ONE LAST TIME.
WHATEVER CRIME YOU THINK WE COMMITTED, YOU HAVE THE WRONG--
Save it. You're both under arrest.
Whatever this box is, they wanted to hold onto it pretty bad and *I want to know why.*
Robot. Pick Batman up. We'll take them both back with us.
Soldier-- listen to me--
THAT'S AN ORDER, MAXIMUM.

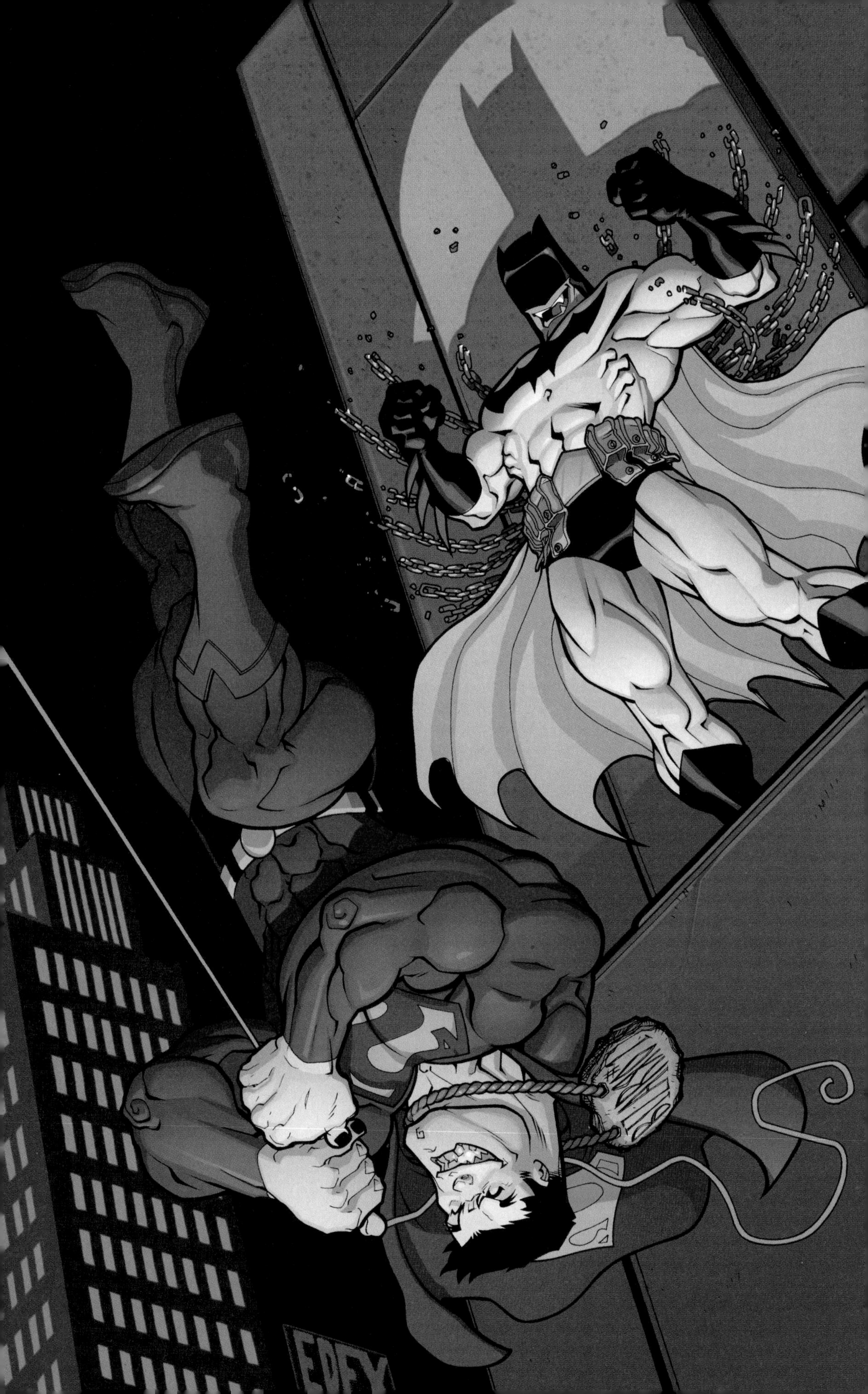

"HEROES AND VILLAINS"

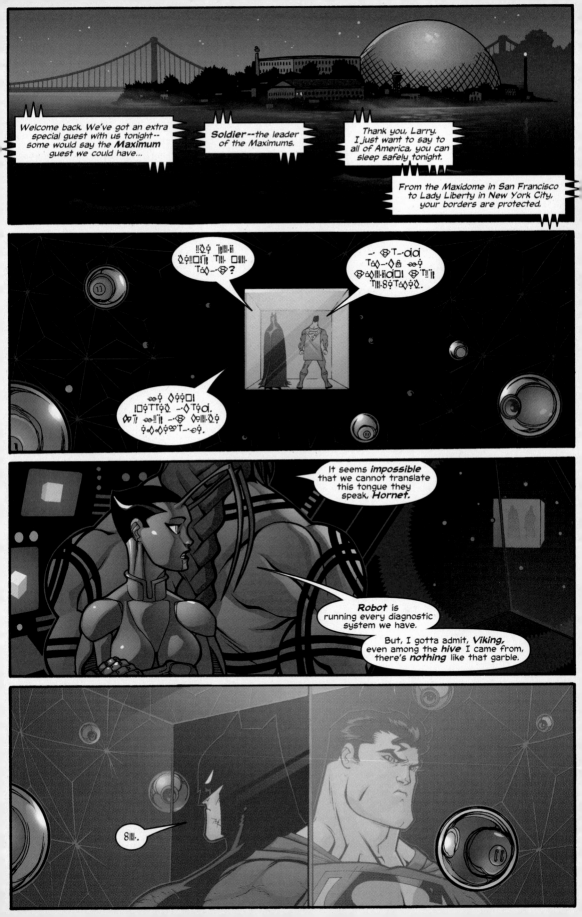

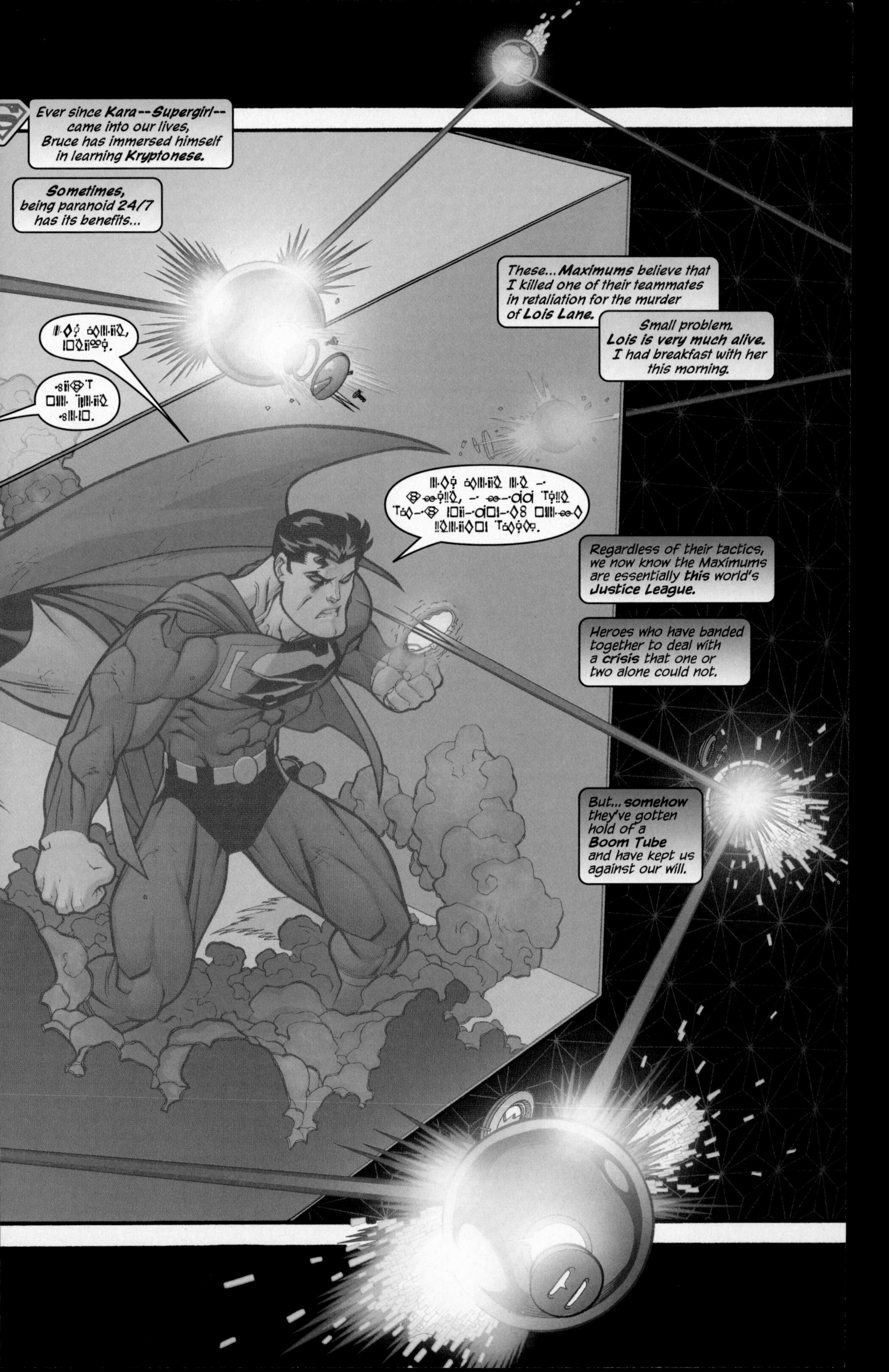
Ever since Kara--Supergirl--came into our lives, Bruce has immersed himself in learning Kryptonese.
Sometimes, being paranoid 24/7 has its benefits...
These... Maximums believe that I killed one of their teammates in retaliation for the murder of Lois Lane.
Small problem. Lois is very much alive. I had breakfast with her this morning.
Regardless of their tactics, we now know the Maximums are essentially this world's Justice League.
Heroes who have banded together to deal with a crisis that one or two alone could not.
But... somehow they've gotten hold of a Boom Tube and have kept us against our will.

Me no am Bizarro #1. This no am The Watchtower, footquarters of the Justice League!

Not with Batzarro, us no am going to rescue our worst idols, Superman and Batman!

KNOCK KNOCK

WHO'S THERE...?

THOOM

GOOD-BYE!

ODD. TRYING TO GET A PSI-READING...

BUT... HIS MIND IS A CACOPHONY OF NOISE.

AS IF A CHILD WERE SPINNING A RADIO DIAL.

BIZARRO. THE IMPERFECT DUPLICATE OF SUPERMAN. ALL THE POWERS AND NONE OF THE INTELLECT.

AS SUCH, INCREDIBLY DANGEROUS. WHAT WOULD HE WANT...HERE?

WRAM

HEY. ME NOT KNOW YOU.

YOU AM MARVIN THE MARTIAN.

YOU AM IN LOVE WITH FIRE!

MARVIN! WHY YOU AM VISIBLE?

ME NOT GO. MUST BE EARLY FOR WHAT ME MUST NOT DO!

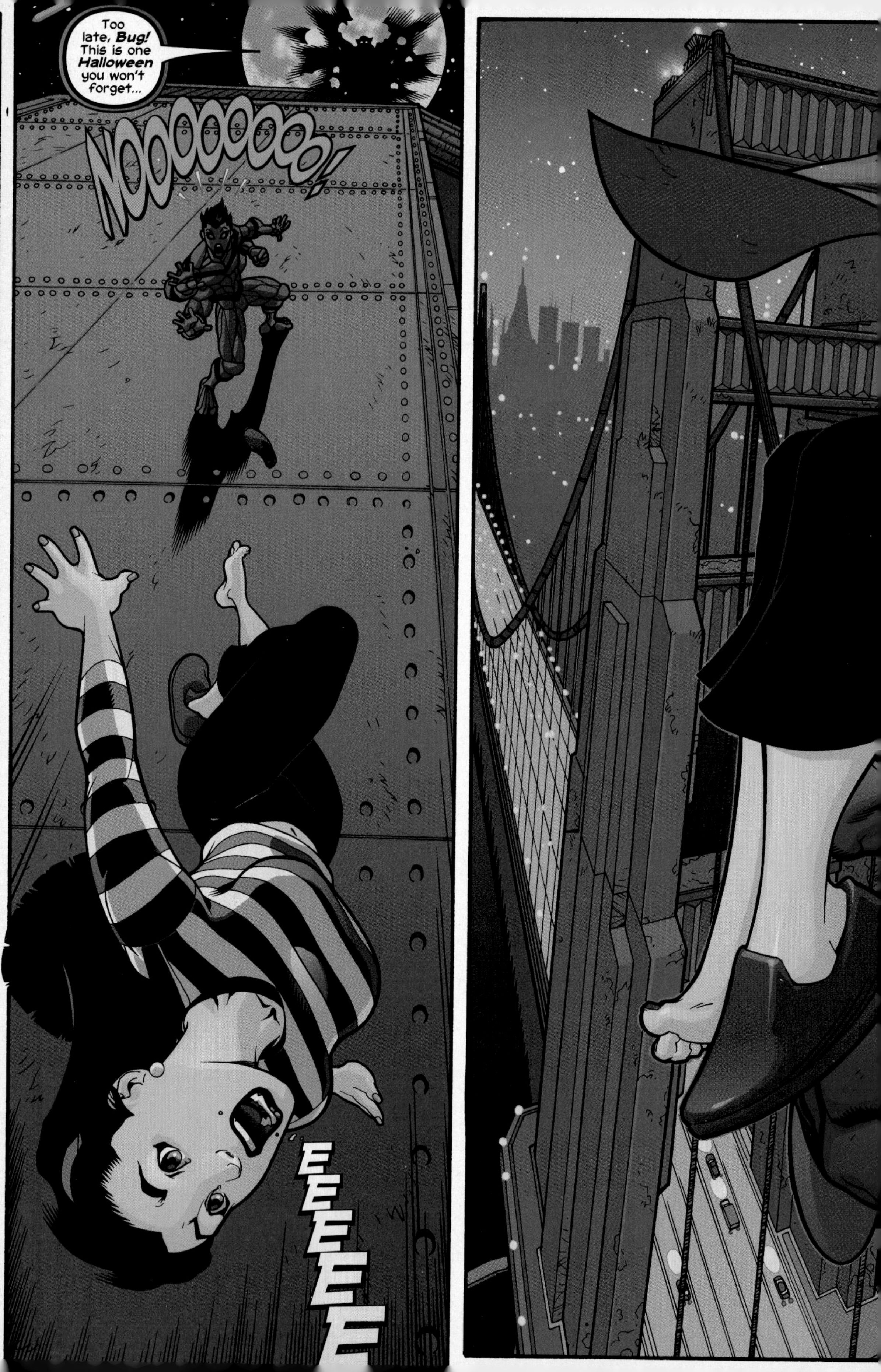

Too late, Bug! This is one Halloween you won't forget...
NOOOOOOOO!
EEEEE

PHTOOM

PHTOOSH

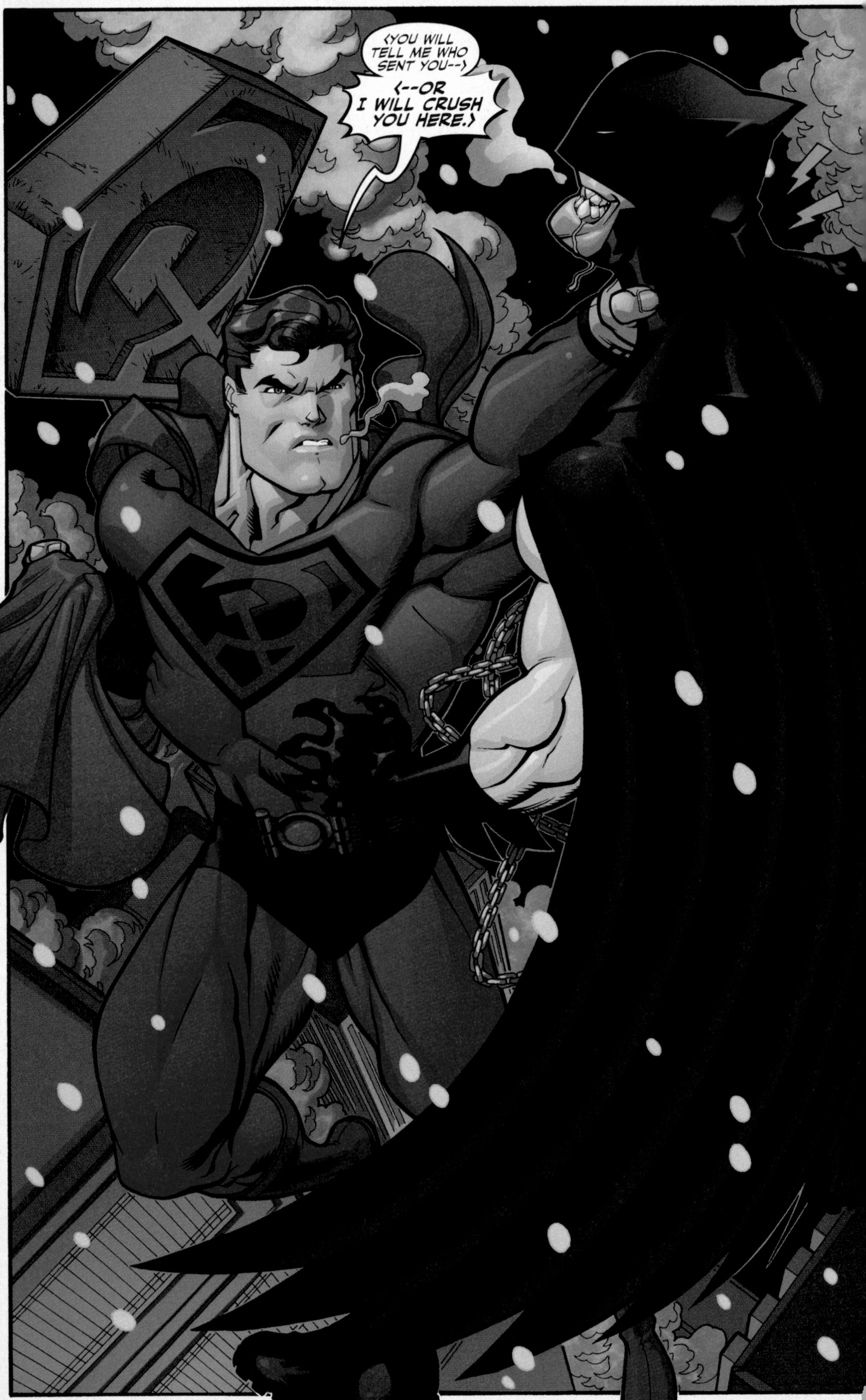
<YOU WILL TELL ME WHO SENT YOU-->
<--OR I WILL CRUSH YOU HERE.>

What's happened to you, Hornet? When I was alive, you never gave a @#$% what Soldier had to say.

You want **vengeance** for Skyscraper or don't you?

You know that answer. Harvey was my one true love. But how do you know what's in this **briefcase** is going to bring down that Superman guy?

And that concludes our show for tonight. Be with us tomorrow night when our guests will be **Freddie Prinze, Jr.** and **Samuel L. Jackson.**

I'm telling you, **Bowman,** I could get kicked out of the Maximums for this.

Lost a lot of blood. Internal hemorrhaging too, I'm sure of it.

I KNOW... WHATEVER OUR DIFFERENCES... BUT IF YOU VALUE *ANYTHING*...

...DO *NOT* OPEN THAT CASE...

Ooops.

Well, it's a little too late now...

YOU DON'T KNOW WHAT {ACKKGH}

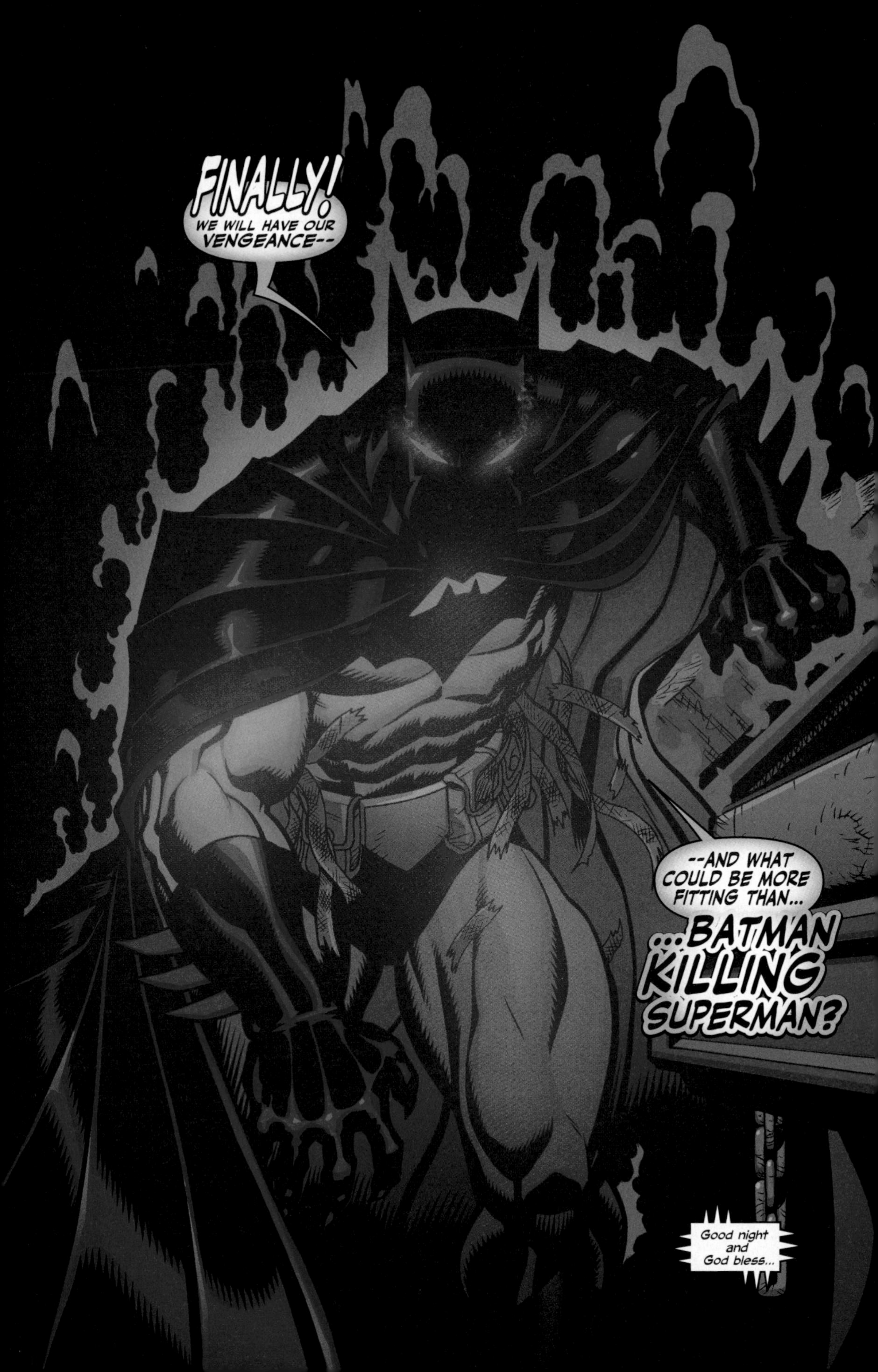
FINALLY! WE WILL HAVE OUR VENGEANCE--
--AND WHAT COULD BE MORE FITTING THAN...
...BATMAN KILLING SUPERMAN?
Good night and God bless...

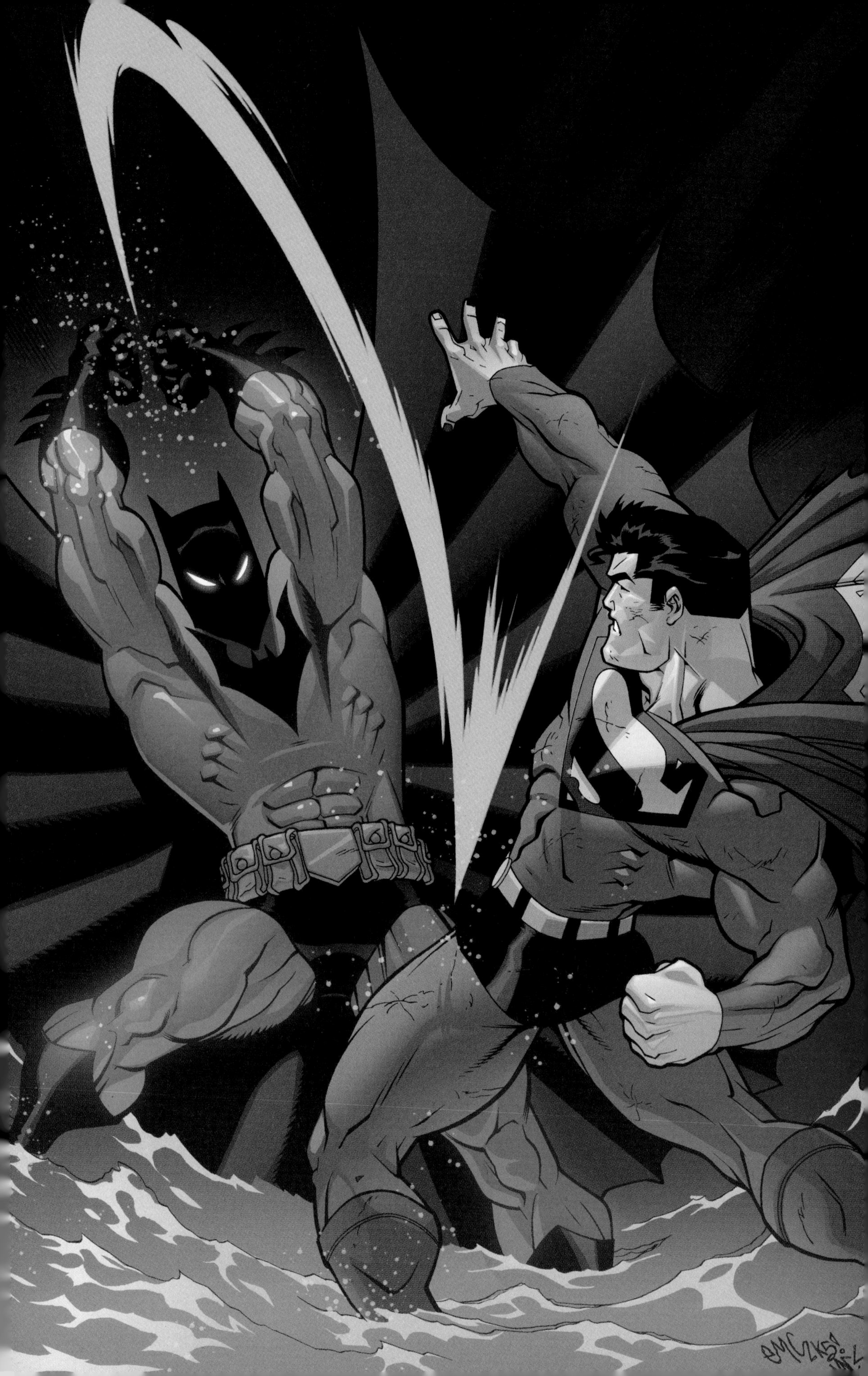

"SMOKE AND MIRRORS"

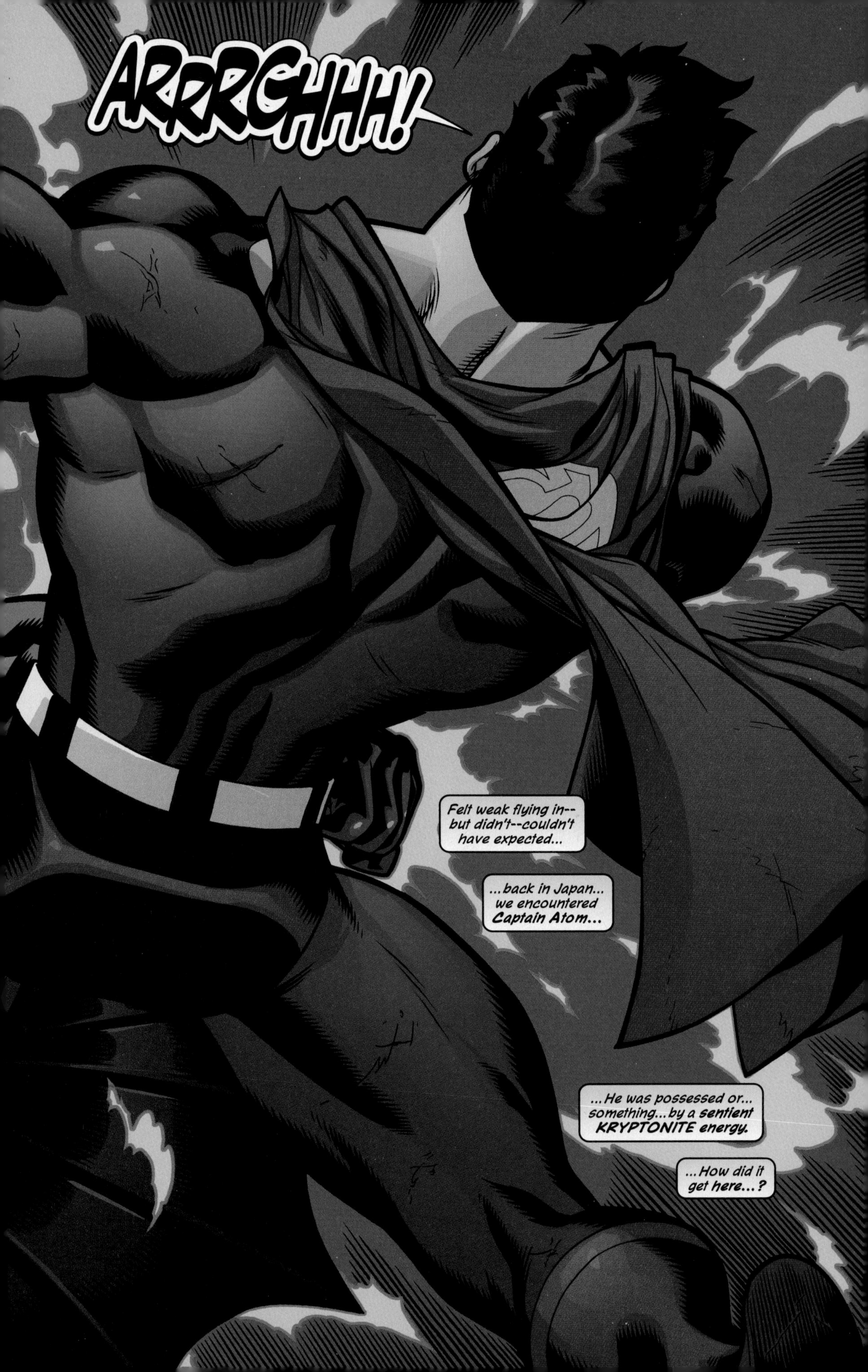
ARRRGHHH!
Felt weak flying in--but didn't--couldn't have expected...
...back in Japan... we encountered Captain Atom...
...He was possessed or... something... by a sentient KRYPTONITE energy.
...How did it get here...?

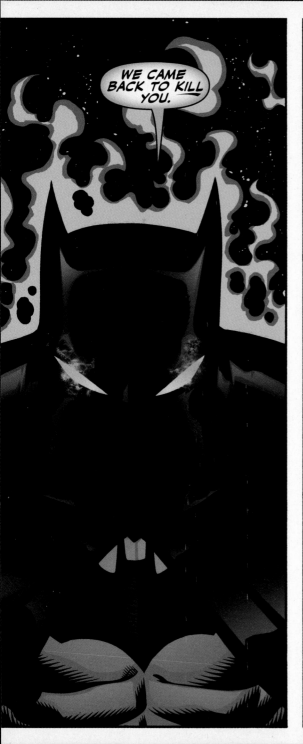

WE CAME BACK TO KILL YOU.

THEN YOU CAME BACK FOR NOTHING.

It wasn't that long ago that our roles were *reversed.* Poison Ivy had taken over my mind and turned me against Bruce.

But... Bruce was prepared. He had a game plan to stop me.

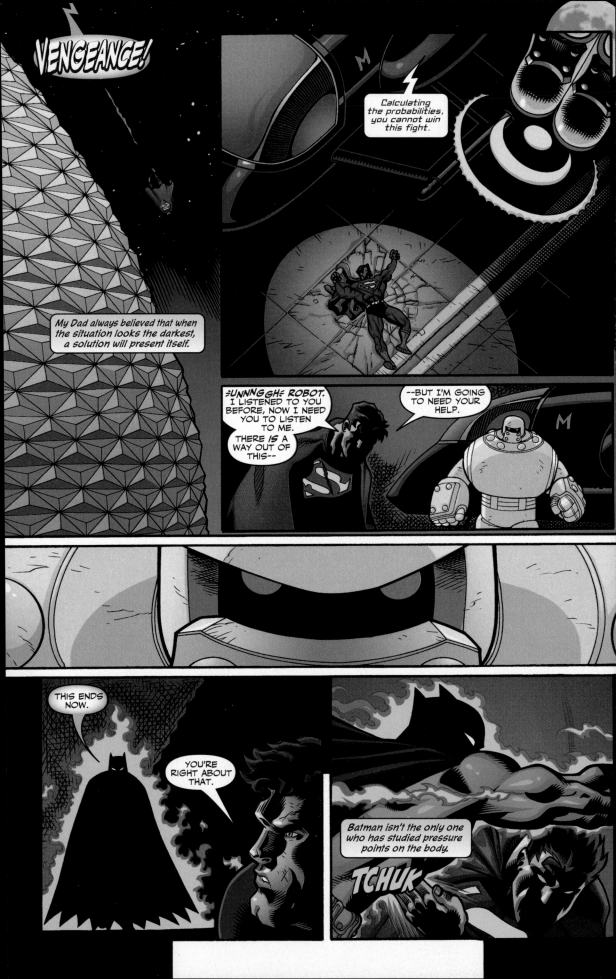

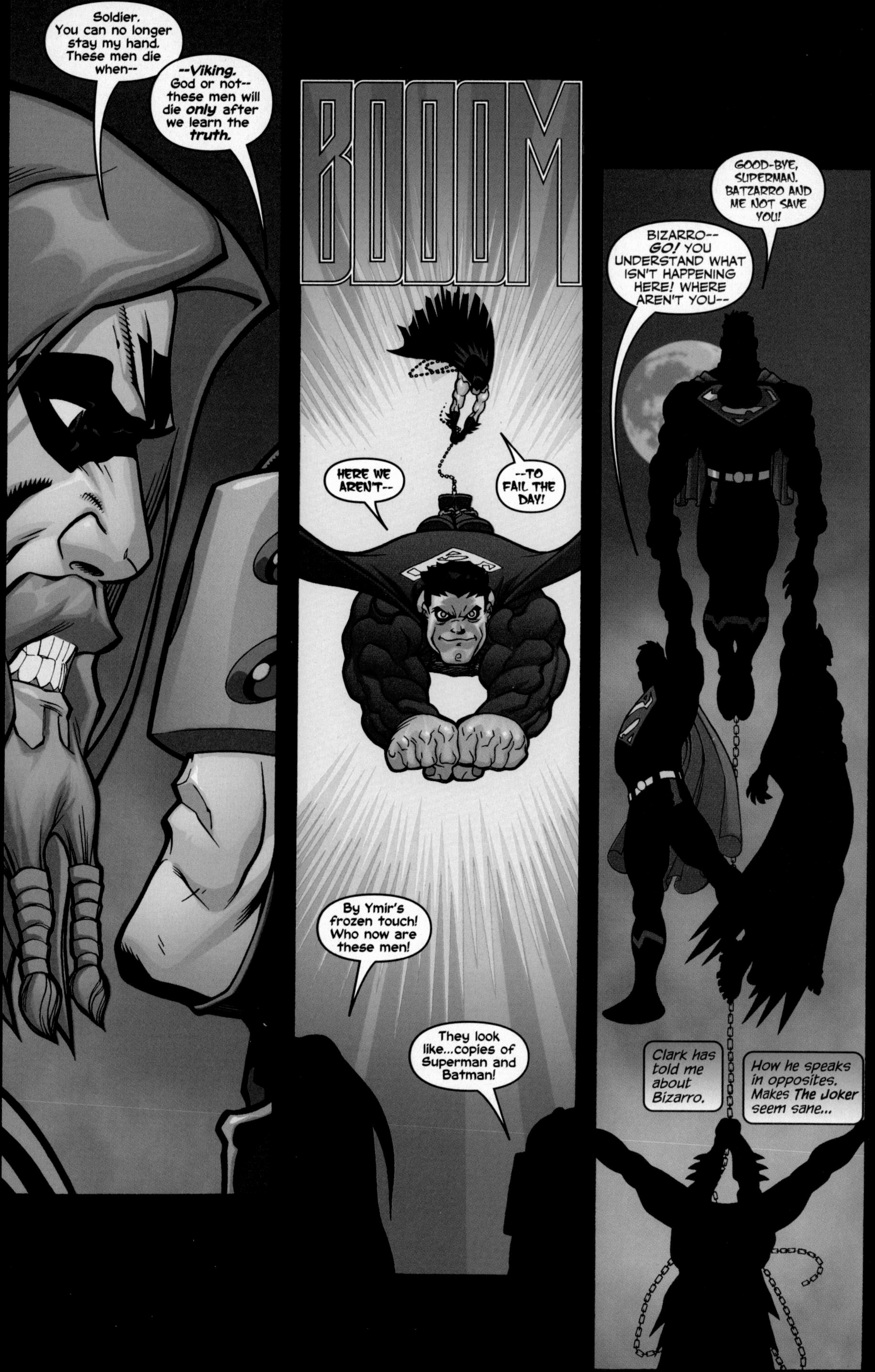

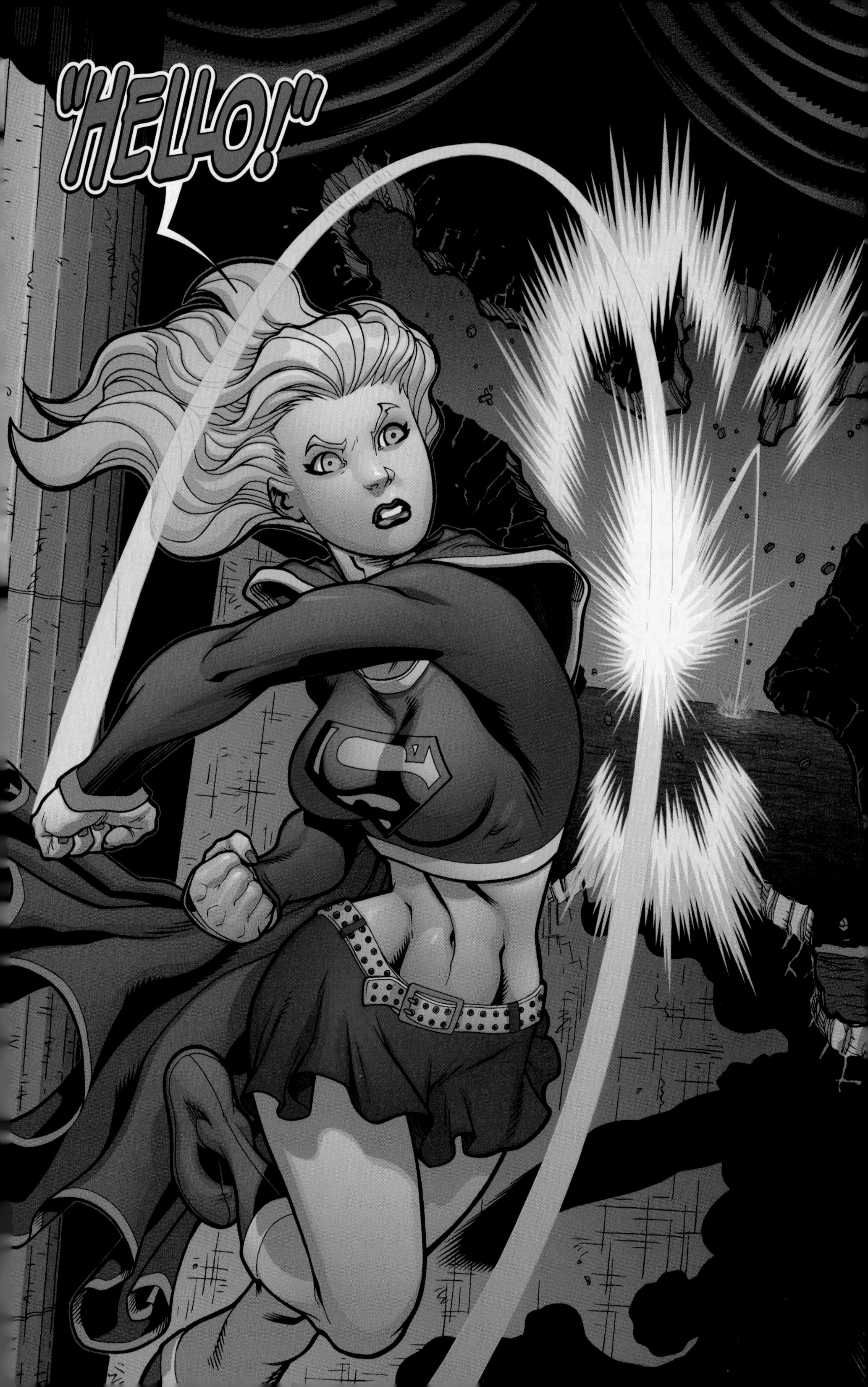
"HELLO!"

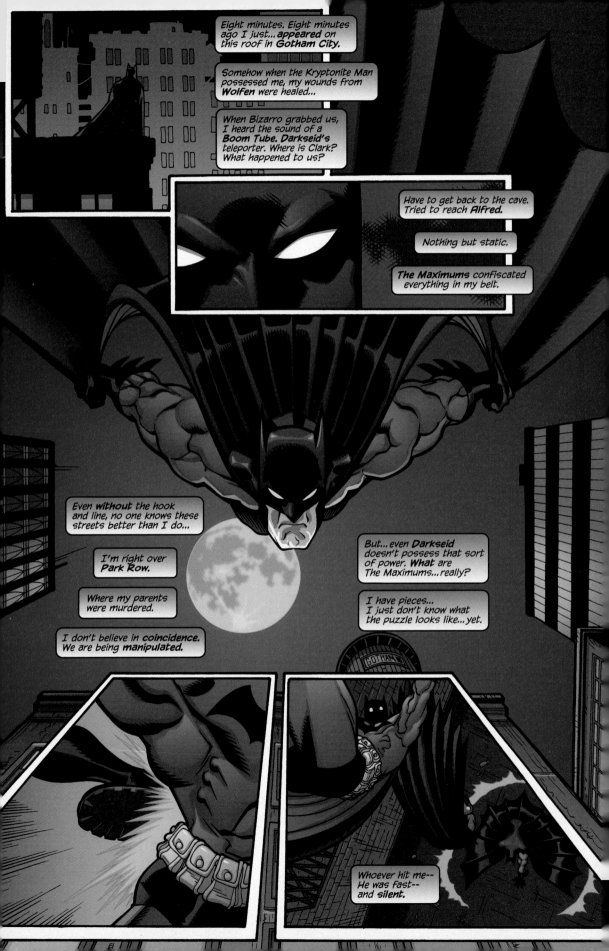

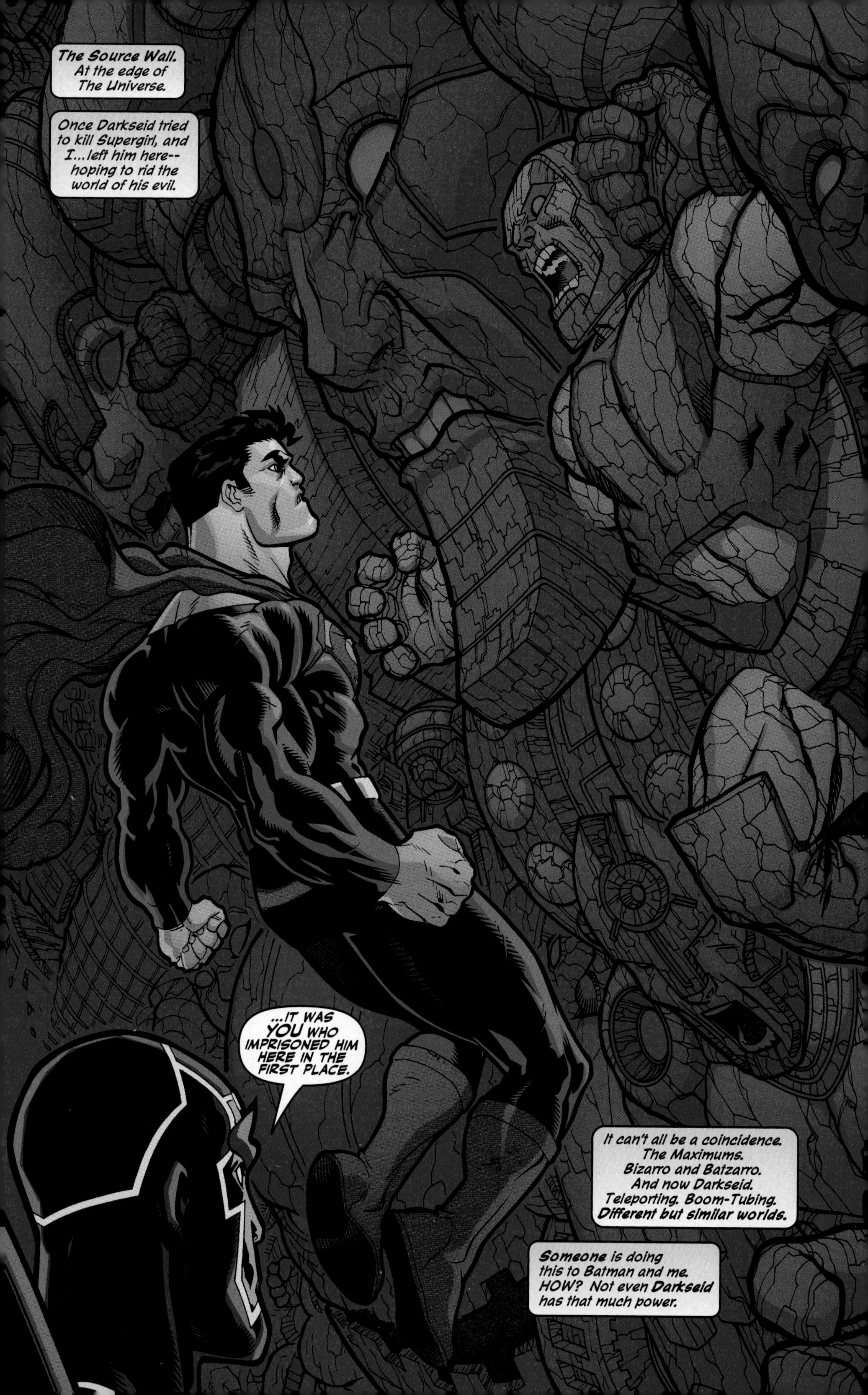
The Source Wall. At the edge of The Universe.
Once Darkseid tried to kill Supergirl, and I...left him here--hoping to rid the world of his evil.
...IT WAS YOU WHO IMPRISONED HIM HERE IN THE FIRST PLACE.
It can't all be a coincidence. The Maximums. Bizarro and Batzarro. And now Darkseid. Teleporting. Boom-Tubing. Different but similar worlds.
Someone is doing this to Batman and me. HOW? Not even Darkseid has that much power.

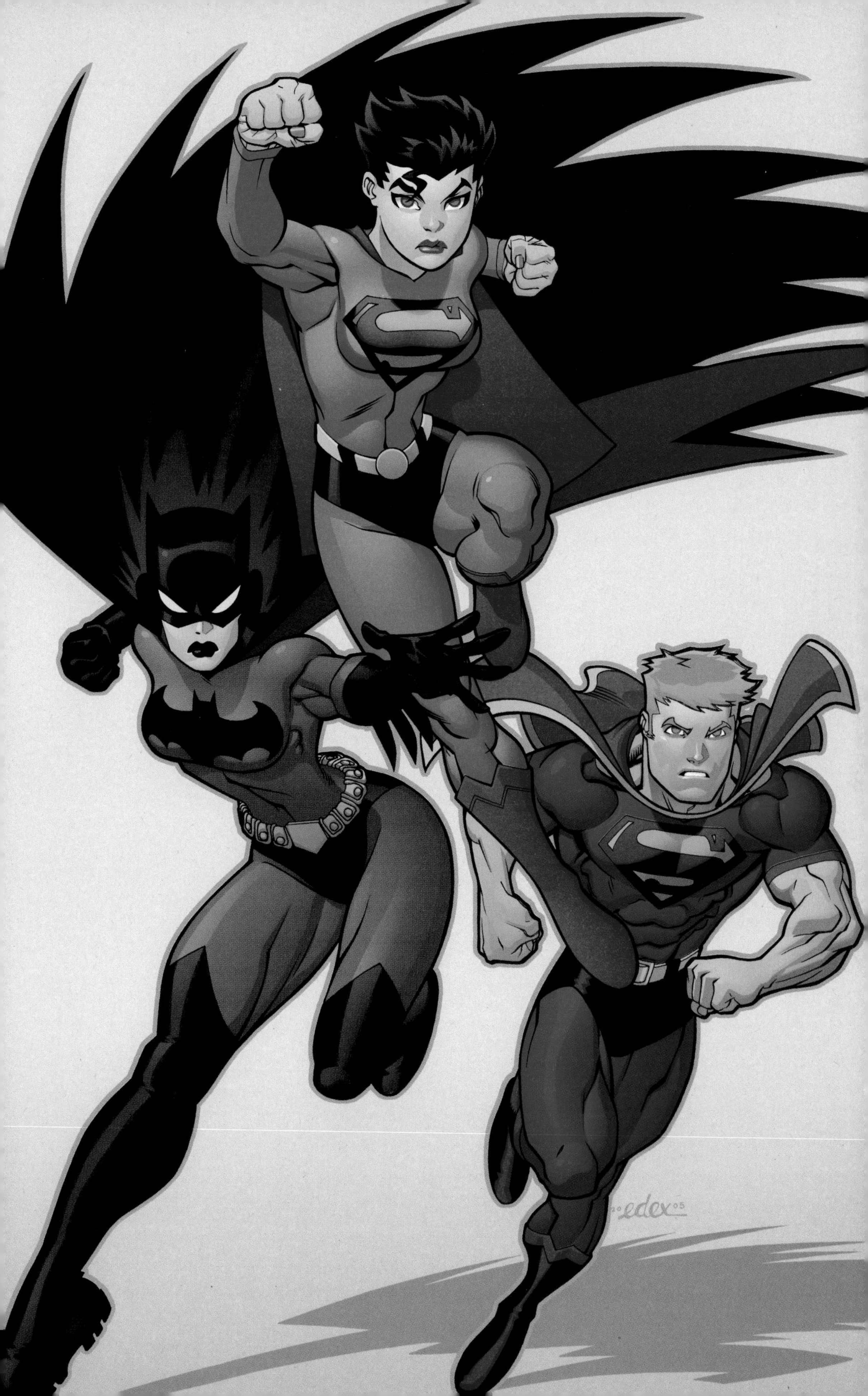

"THE PRICE OF OUR SINS"

As... impossible... or absurd as it sounds, in a future that now never existed, Batman and I were... criminals.
Despots who ruled Earth and slaughtered anyone who didn't obey us.
It was as though we'd been raised by Darkseid himself.
It was then, with more than a hint of irony, that Darkseid would be crucial in restoring things to the way they should be.
He did so for a price. One he did not name at the time.

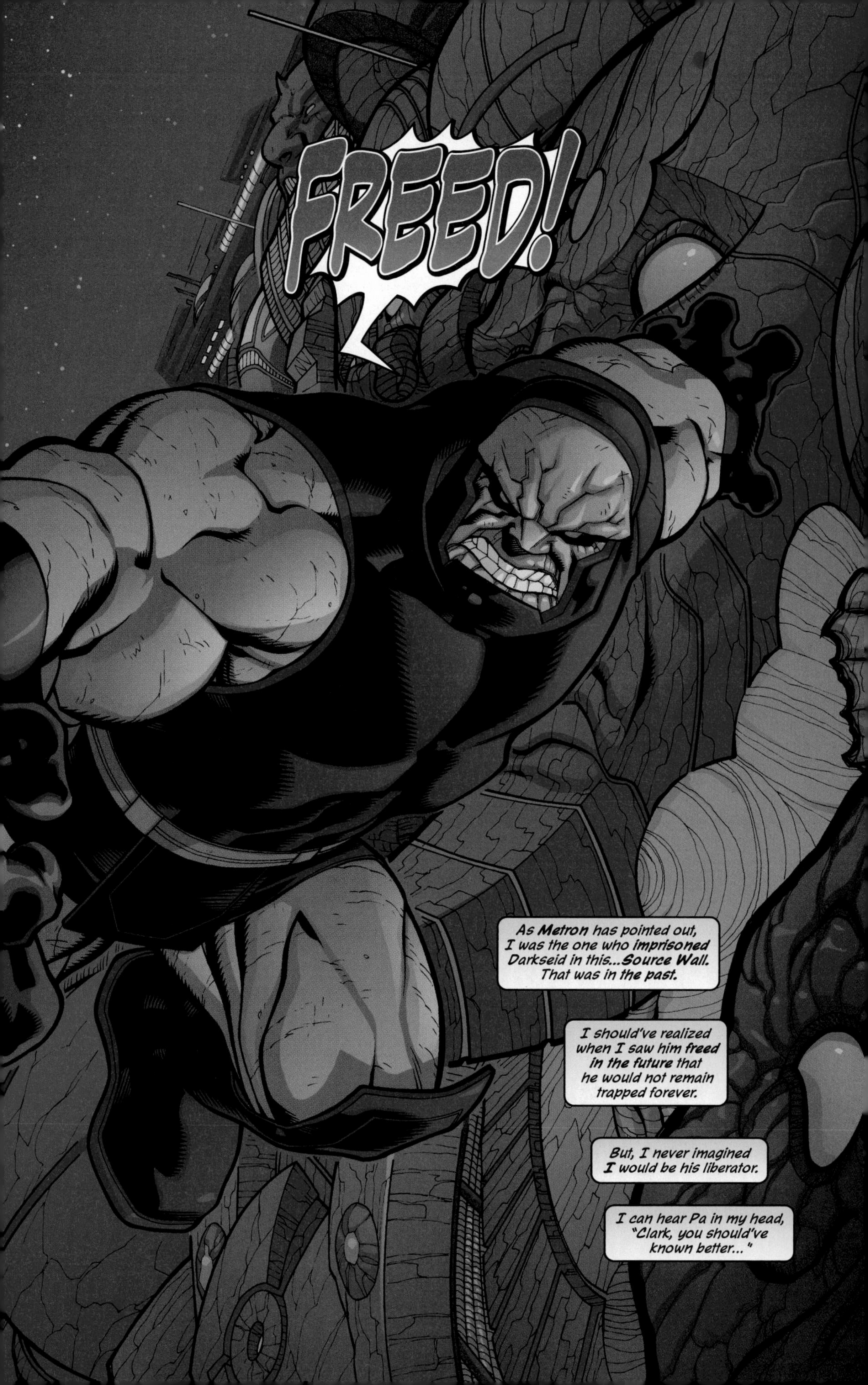
FREED!
As Metron has pointed out, I was the one who imprisoned Darkseid in this...Source Wall. That was in the past.
I should've realized when I saw him freed in the future that he would not remain trapped forever.
But, I never imagined I would be his liberator.
I can hear Pa in my head, "Clark, you should've known better..."

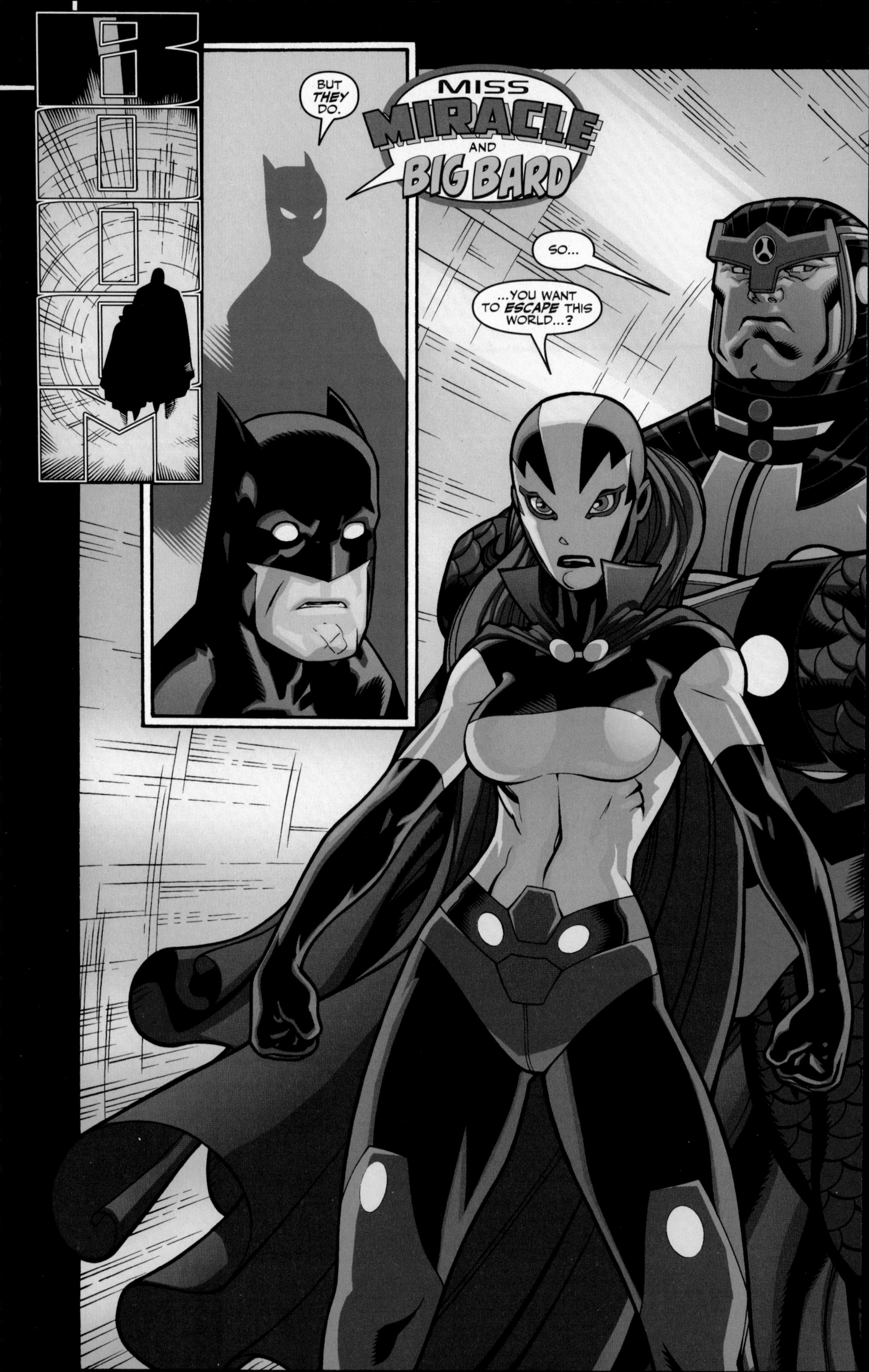
BOOM
BUT THEY DO.
MISS MIRACLE AND BIG BARD
SO...
...YOU WANT TO ESCAPE THIS WORLD...?

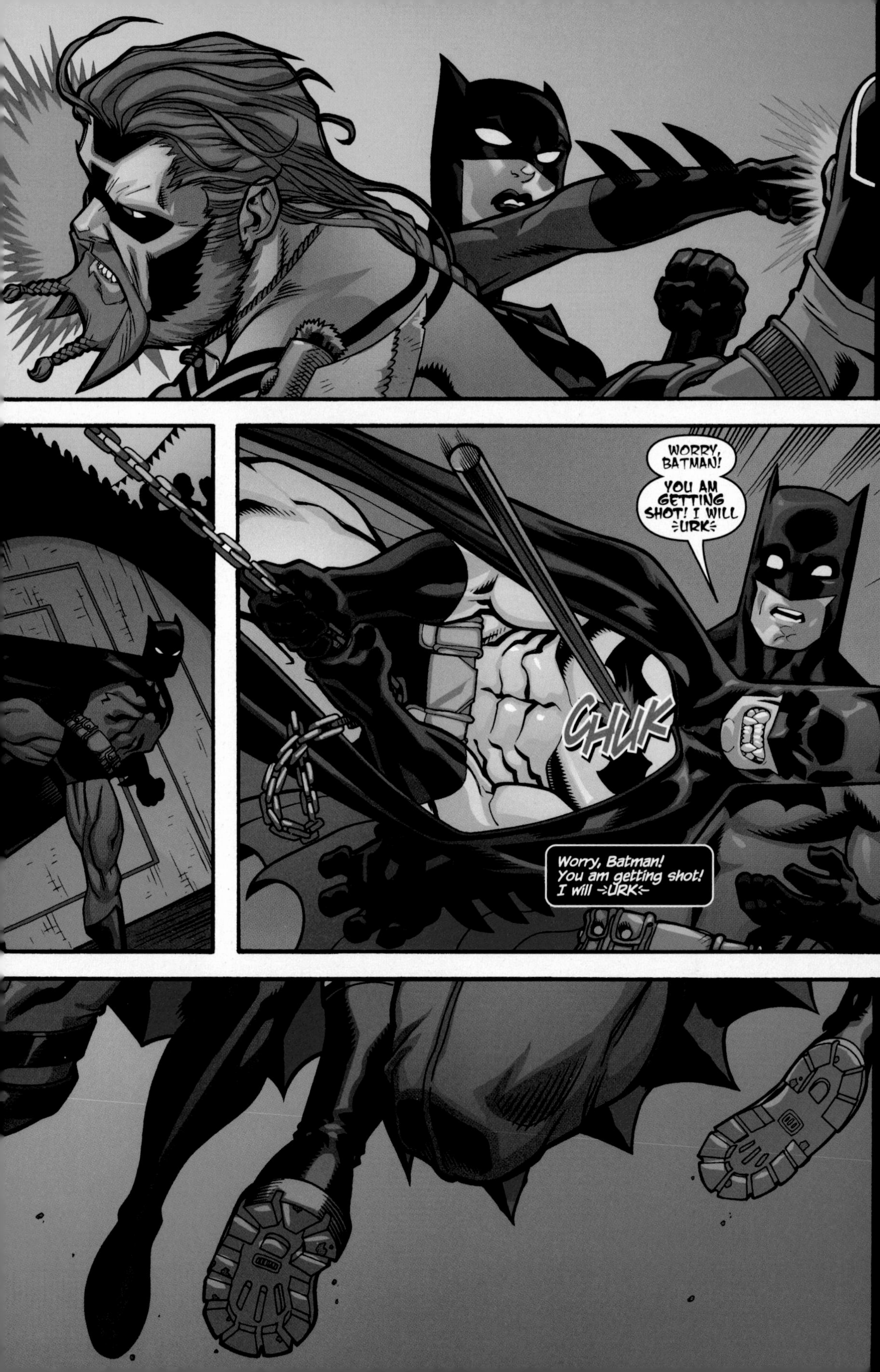
WORRY, BATMAN!
YOU AM GETTING SHOT! I WILL URK
CHUK
Worry, Batman! You am getting shot! I will URK

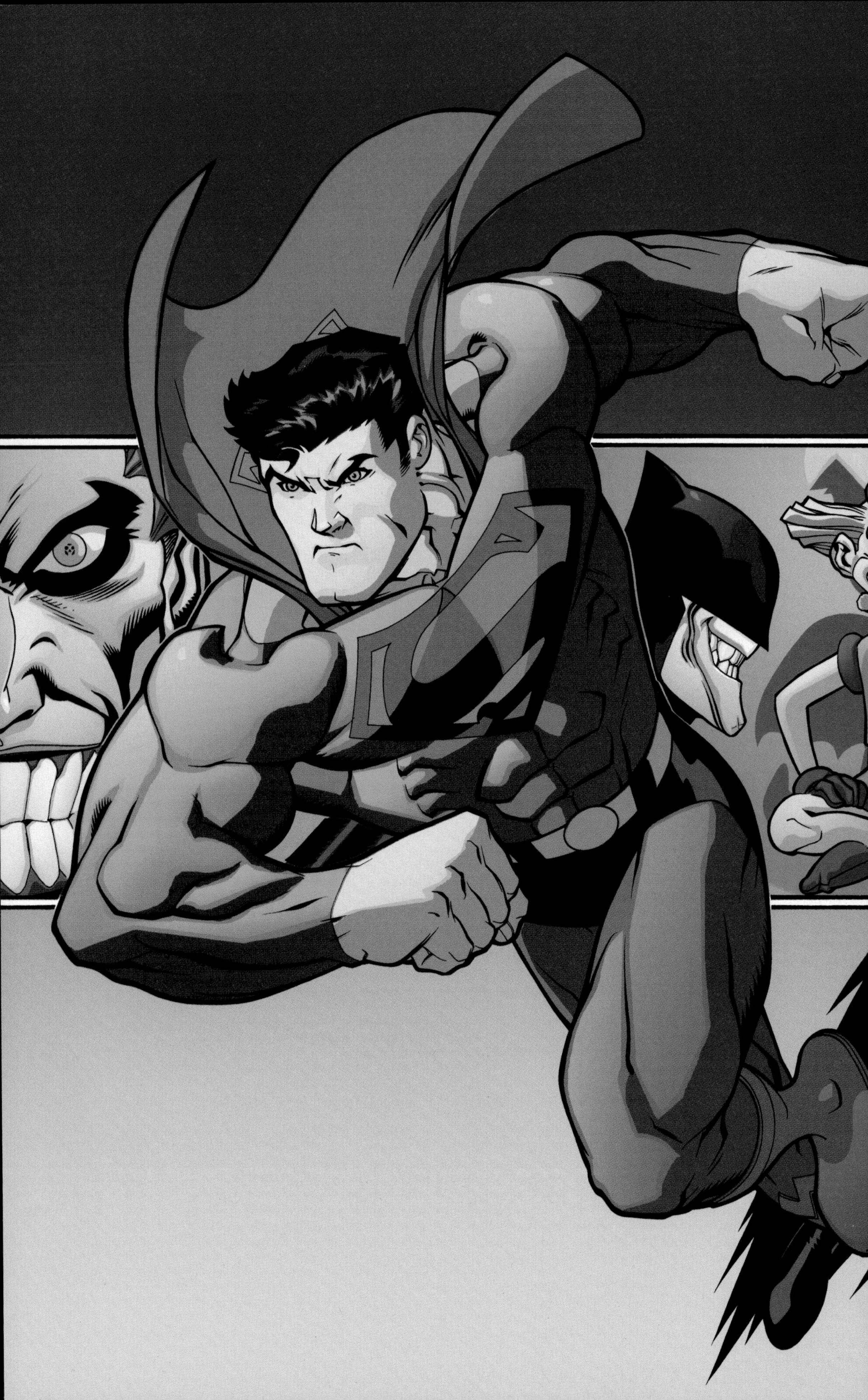

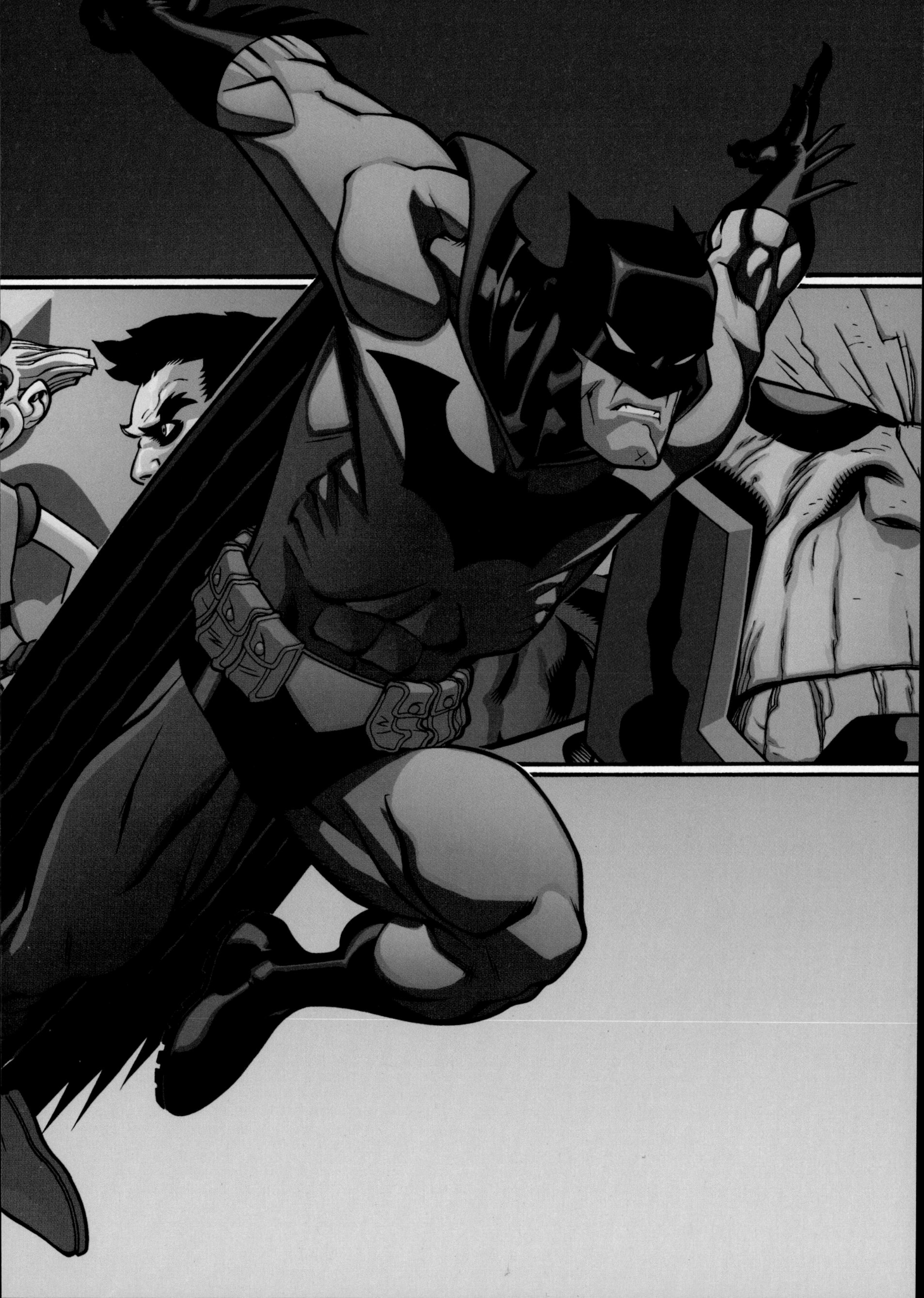

"SUPERMEN / BATMEN"

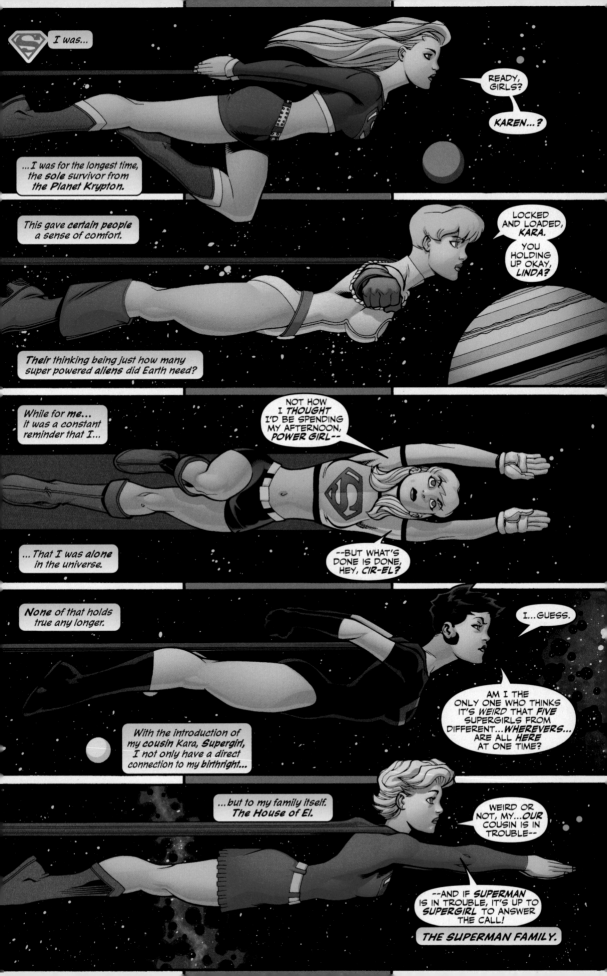

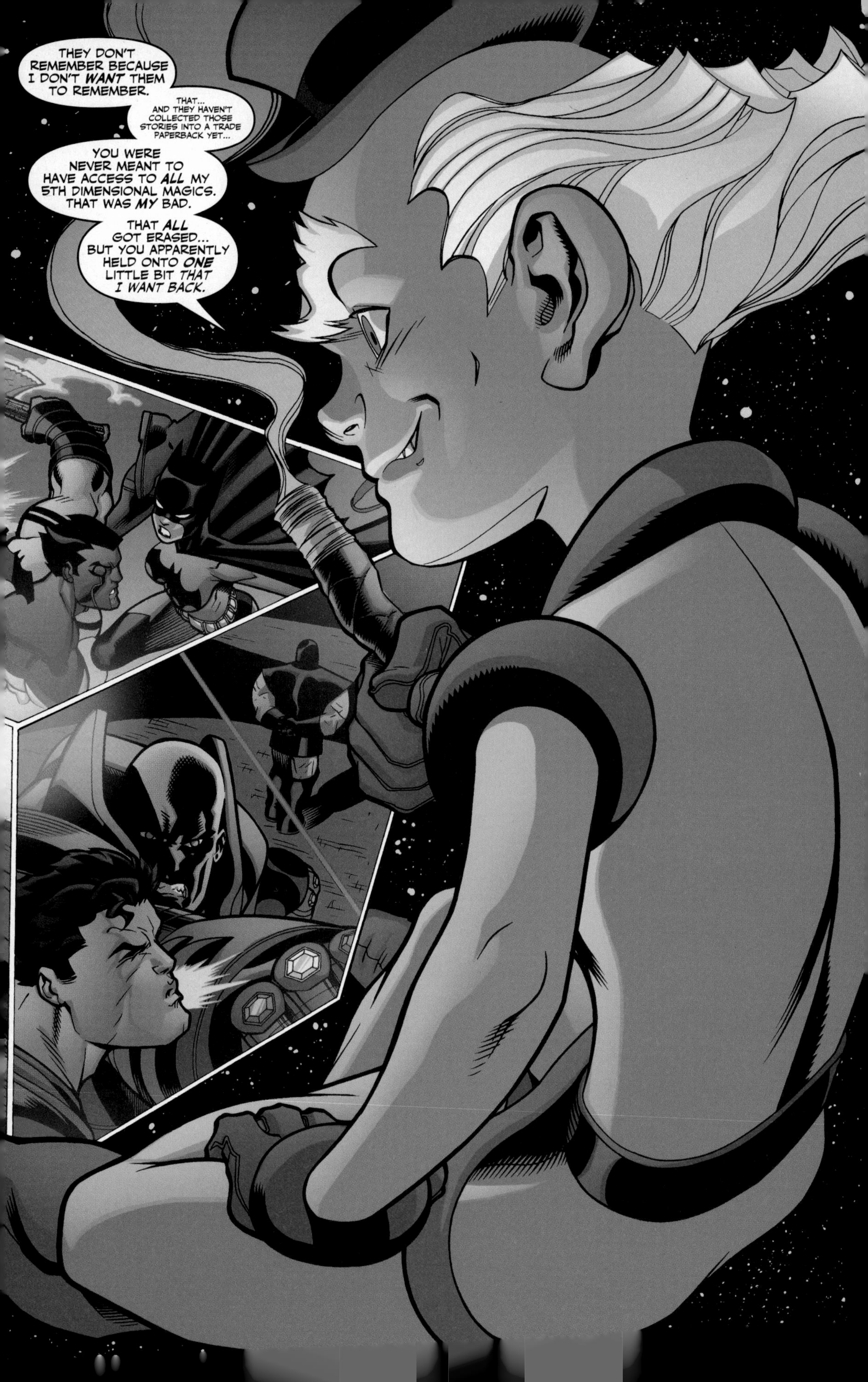
THEY DON'T REMEMBER BECAUSE I DON'T *WANT* THEM TO REMEMBER.
THAT... AND THEY HAVEN'T COLLECTED THOSE STORIES INTO A TRADE PAPERBACK YET...
YOU WERE NEVER MEANT TO HAVE ACCESS TO *ALL* MY 5TH DIMENSIONAL MAGICS. THAT WAS *MY* BAD.
THAT *ALL* GOT ERASED... BUT YOU APPARENTLY HELD ONTO *ONE* LITTLE BIT *THAT I WANT BACK.*

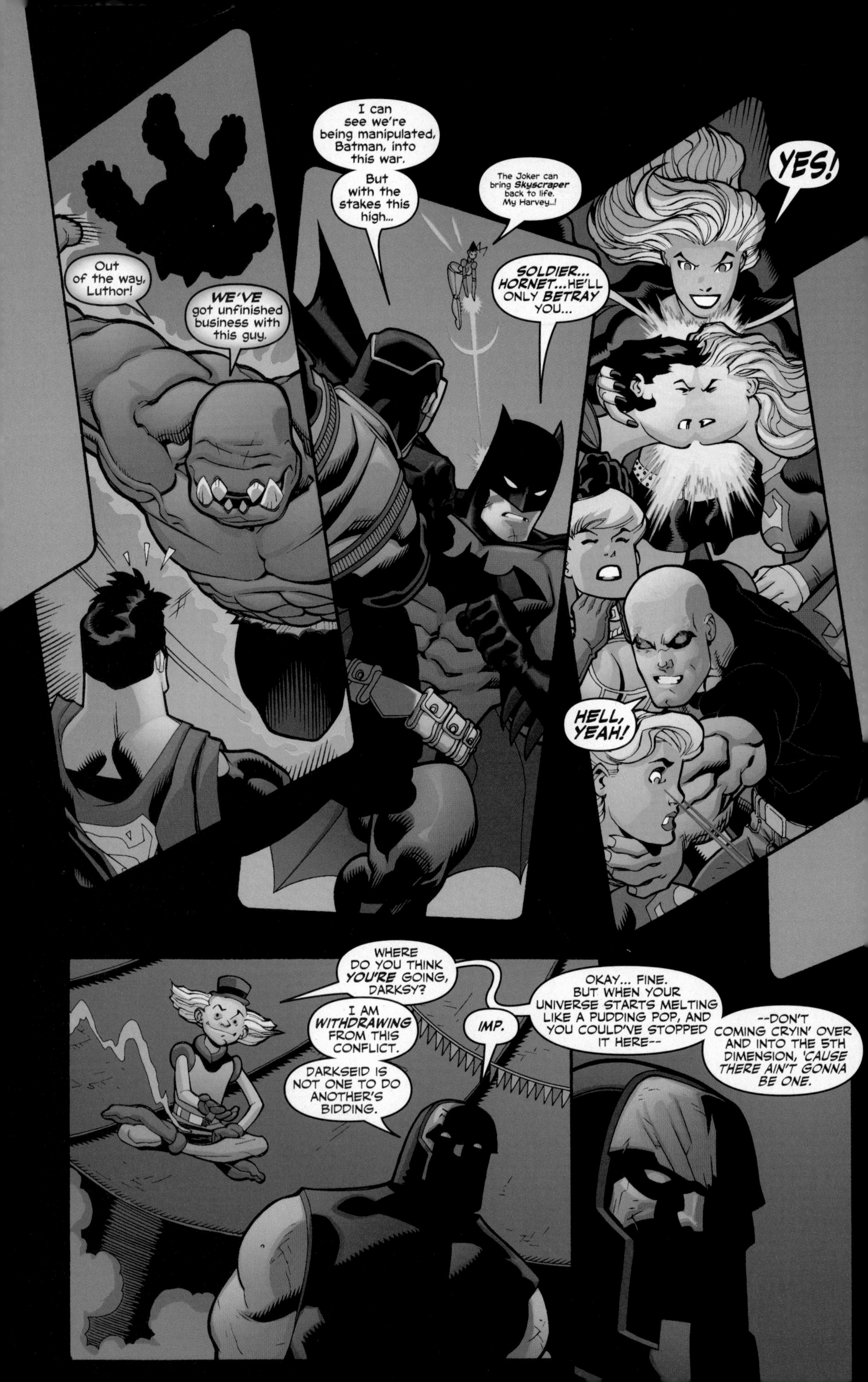
Out of the way, Luthor!
WE'VE got unfinished business with this guy.
I can see we're being manipulated, Batman, into this war.
But with the stakes this high...
The Joker can bring Skyscraper back to life. My Harvey...!
SOLDIER... HORNET... HE'LL ONLY BETRAY YOU...
YES!
HELL, YEAH!
WHERE DO YOU THINK YOU'RE GOING, DARKSY?
I AM WITHDRAWING FROM THIS CONFLICT.
DARKSEID IS NOT ONE TO DO ANOTHER'S BIDDING.
IMP.
OKAY... FINE. BUT WHEN YOUR UNIVERSE STARTS MELTING LIKE A PUDDING POP, AND YOU COULD'VE STOPPED IT HERE--
--DON'T COMING CRYIN' OVER AND INTO THE 5TH DIMENSION, 'CAUSE THERE AIN'T GONNA BE ONE.

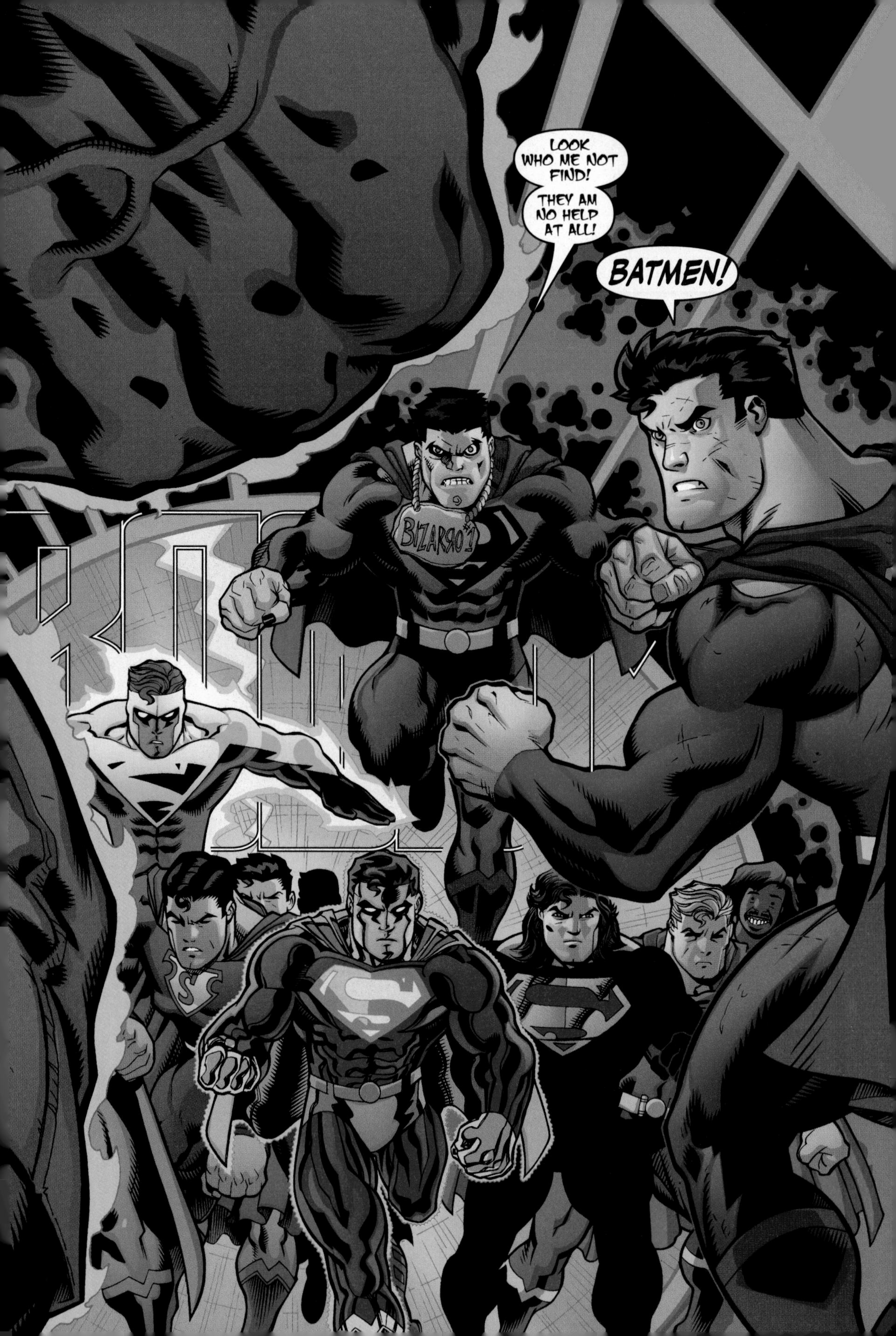
LOOK WHO ME NOT FIND!
THEY AM NO HELP AT ALL!
BATMEN!
BIZARRO 1

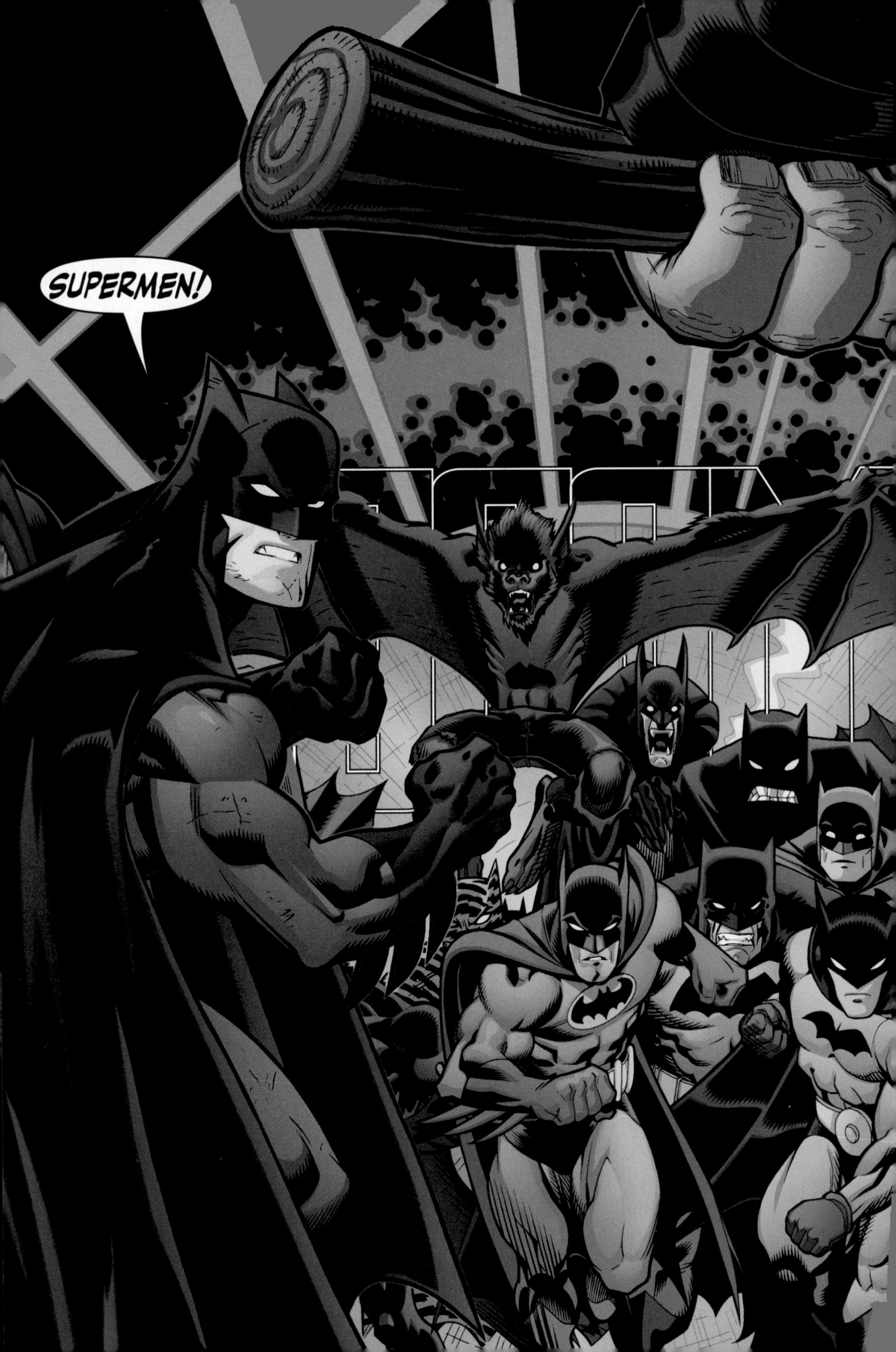
SUPERMEN!

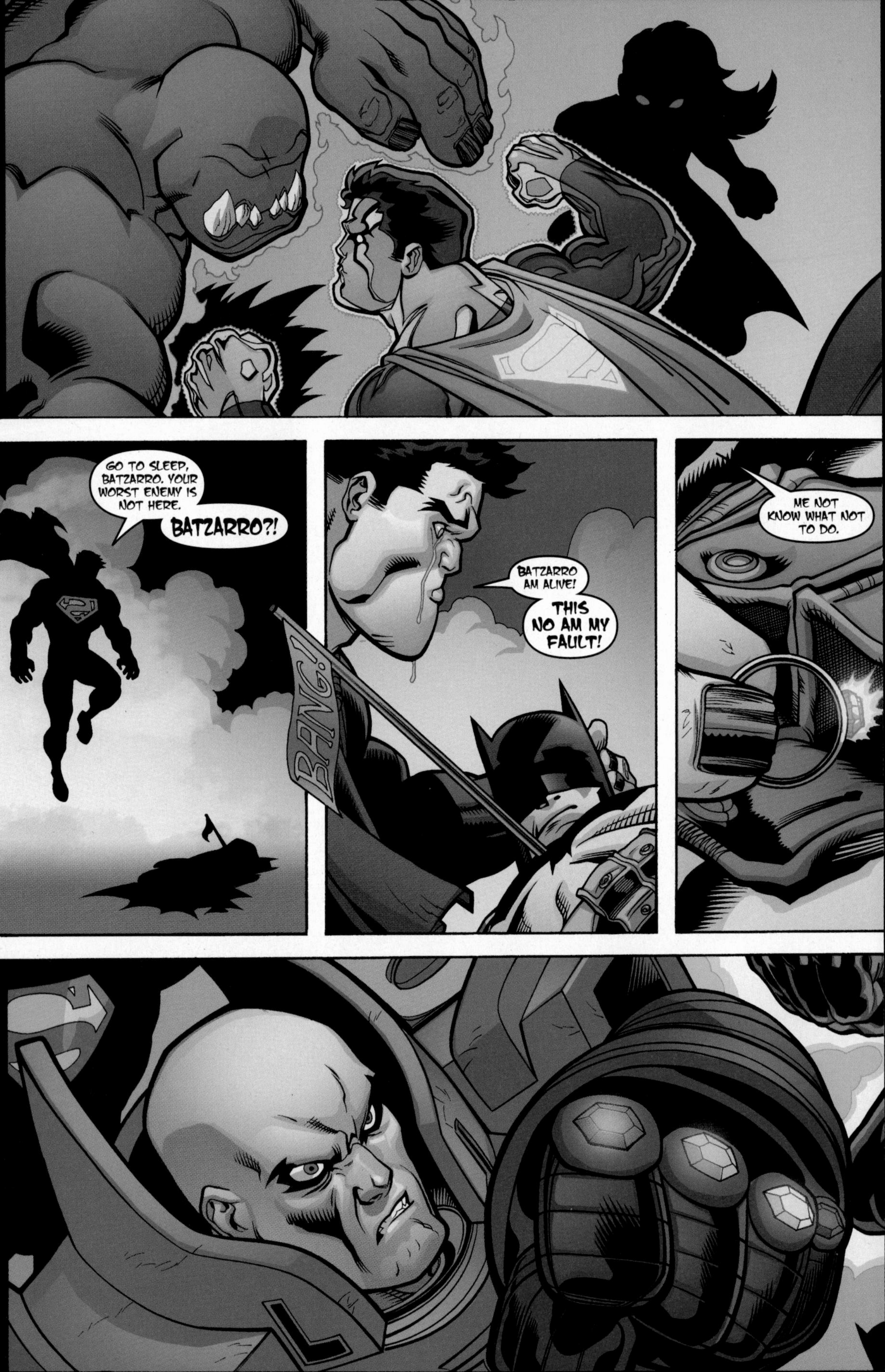
GO TO SLEEP, BATZARRO. YOUR WORST ENEMY IS NOT HERE.
BATZARRO?!
BATZARRO AM ALIVE!
THIS NO AM MY FAULT!
BANG!
ME NOT KNOW WHAT NOT TO DO.

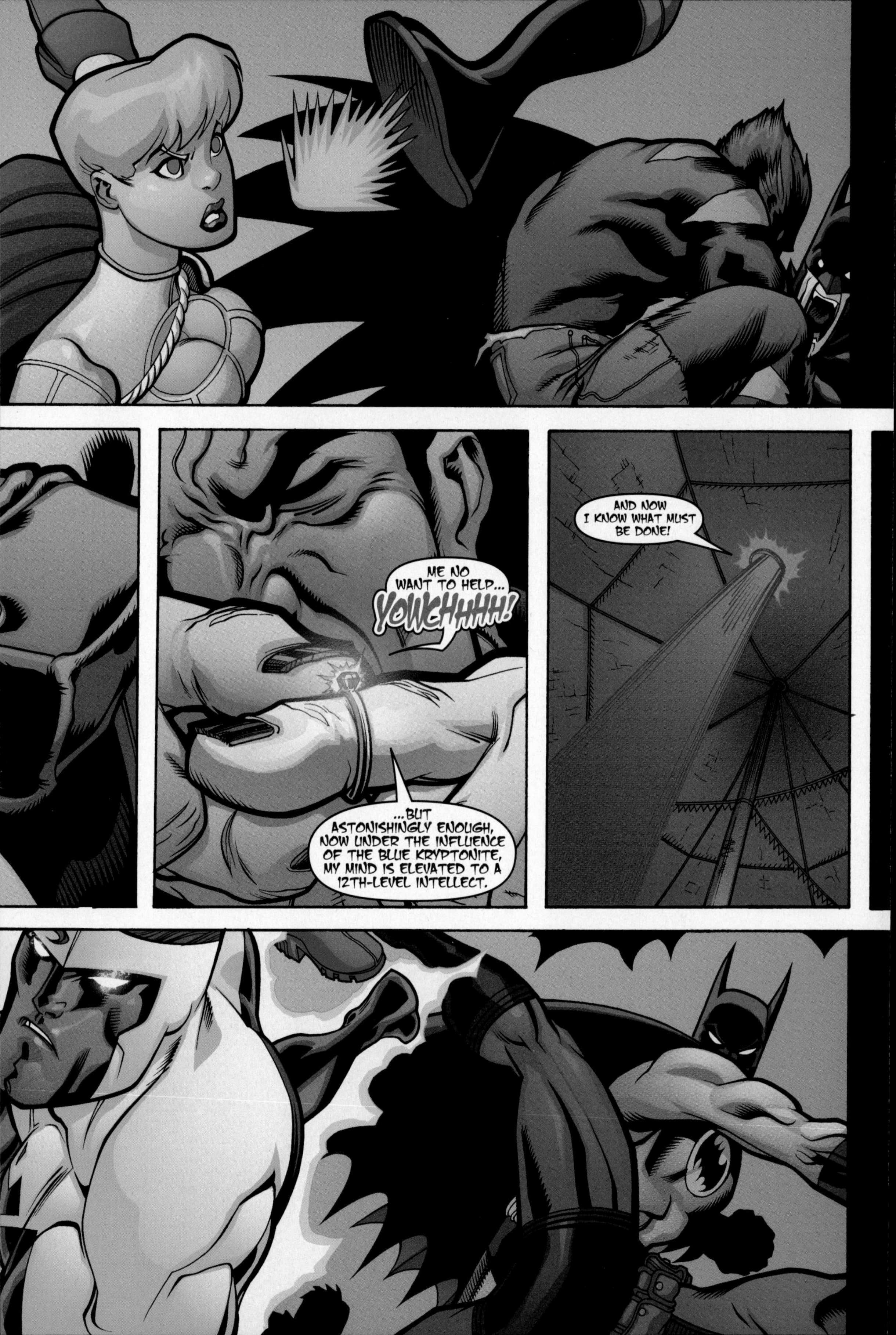
ME NO WANT TO HELP... YOWCHHHH!
...BUT ASTONISHINGLY ENOUGH, NOW UNDER THE INFLUENCE OF THE BLUE KRYPTONITE, MY MIND IS ELEVATED TO A 12TH-LEVEL INTELLECT.
AND NOW I KNOW WHAT MUST BE DONE!

I can't help but think about what has happened to us in the past months.

Luthor's fall from Presidency. Supergirl's arrival. Our lives turned evil. And now...The Maximums...

And through it all, Batman-- Bruce was by my side.

He made a promise on the grave of his parents that he would rid the city of the evil that took their lives.

He'd never admit it, but... Sometimes, it's more than the city. Sometimes, it's the universe.

Maybe that's why we've moved on from enemies to allies to friends...

Maybe.

As a detective, I cannot help but look for patterns. Events that coincide for a reason.

I know that Superman-- Clark doesn't think like I do.

Taking Luthor down. Trusting Supergirl. Seeing my parents die again. And now...JUST how powerful was the Joker?

But the mission-- what he calls "The Never-Ending Battle"...

That is where we meet dead center.

Maybe that is what we base our... relationship on... whatever that may be.

Maybe...

IMP. THIS... CRISIS YOU SPEAK OF. WHAT ROLE DO I PLAY?

YOU DON'T. WE...HAVE A FUTURE TOGETHER THAT HAS YET TO BE REVEALED.

TOGETHER...?

"FROM THE FOURTH WORLD... INTO THE FIFTH DIMENSION!"

KINDA LIKE THAT RING TONE, BIG D.

BOOOM

THE END

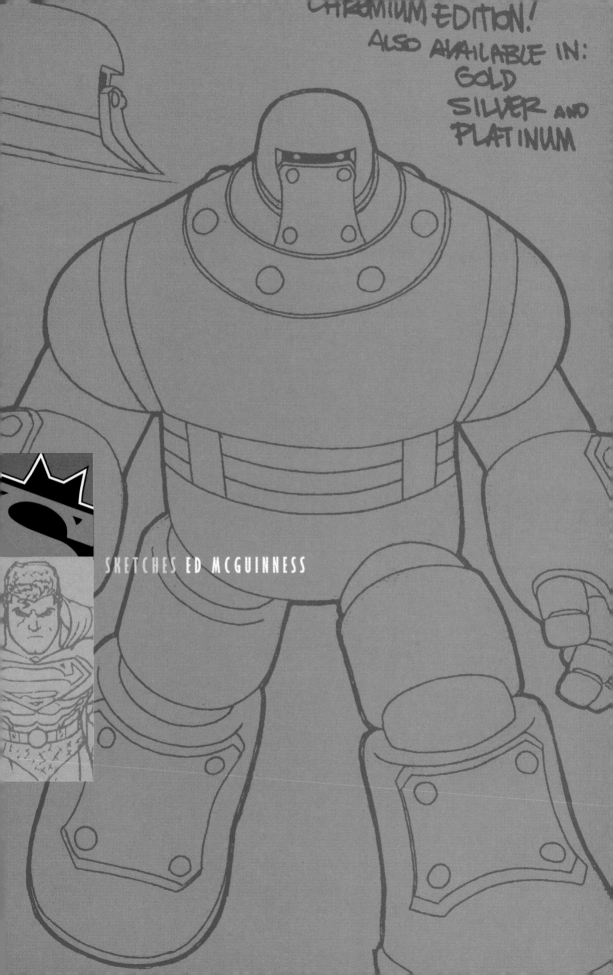

CHROMIUM EDITION!
ALSO AVAILABLE IN:
GOLD
SILVER and
PLATINUM

SKETCHES ED MCGUINNESS

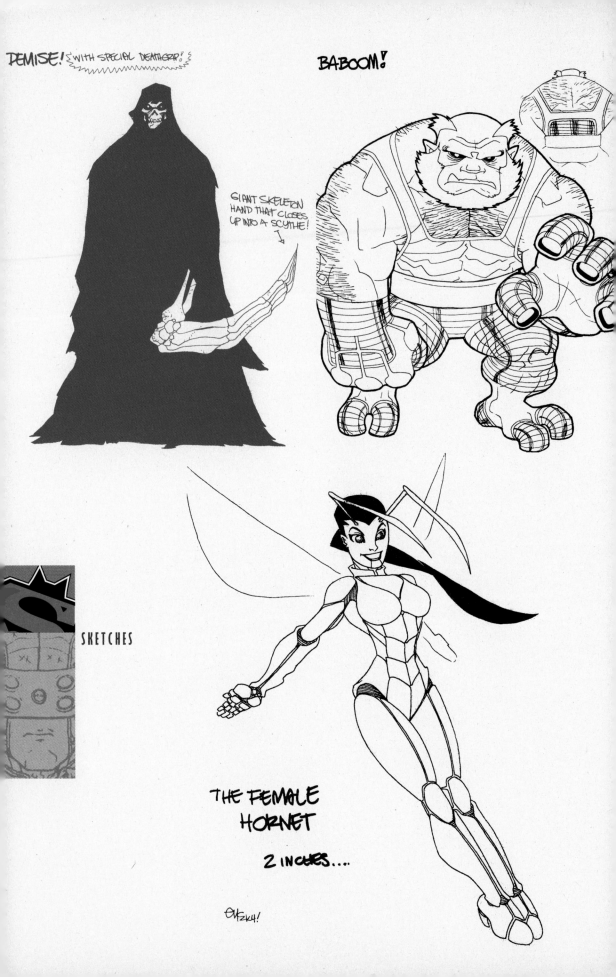

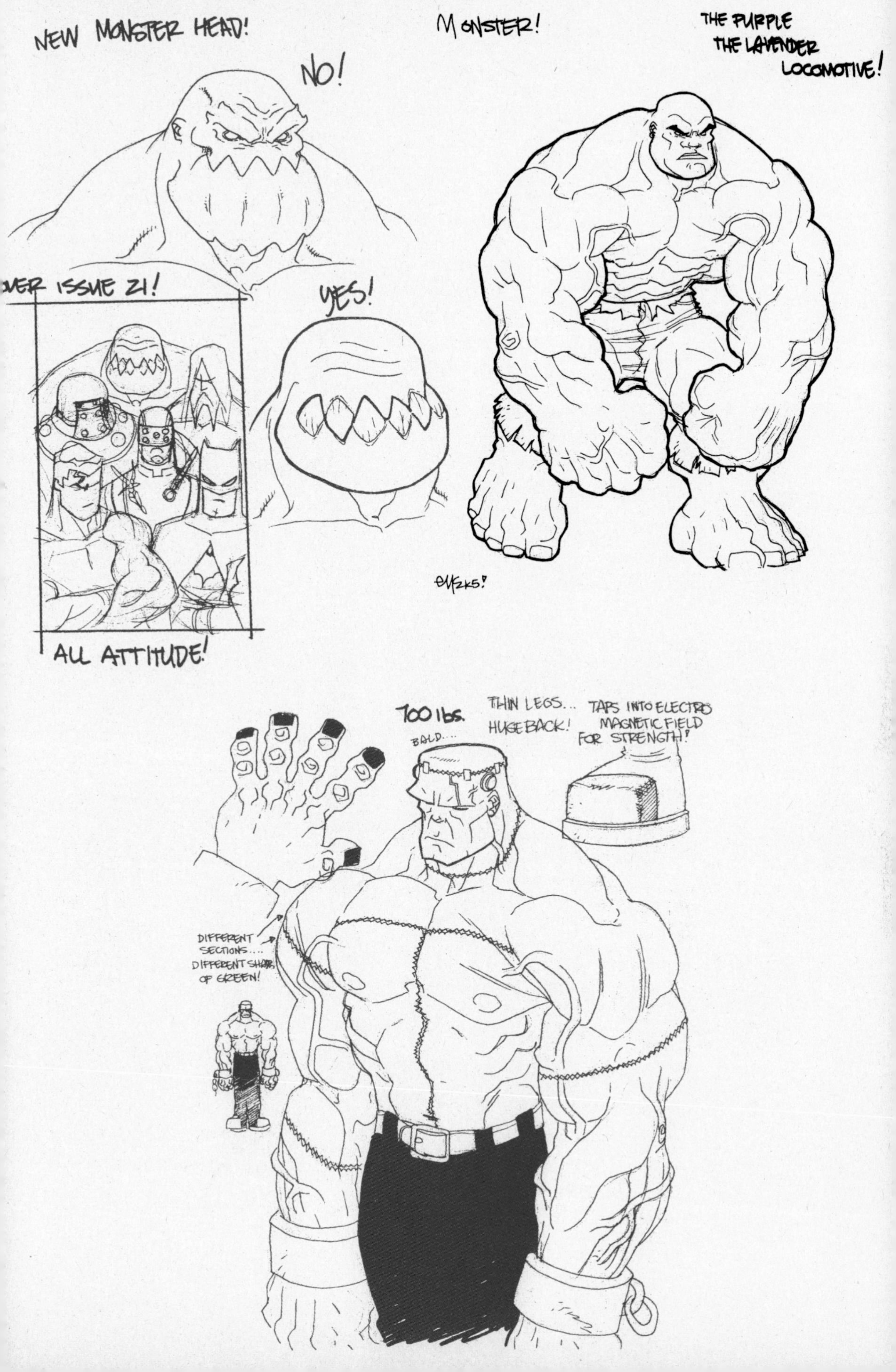

NEW MONSTER HEAD!
NO!
MONSTER!
THE PURPLE
THE LAVENDER
LOCOMOTIVE!
VER ISSUE 21!
YES!
ALL ATTITUDE!
700 lbs.
BALD....
THIN LEGS... HUGE BACK!
TAPS INTO ELECTRO MAGNETIC FIELD FOR STRENGTH!
DIFFERENT SECTIONS.... DIFFERENT SHADE OF GREEN!

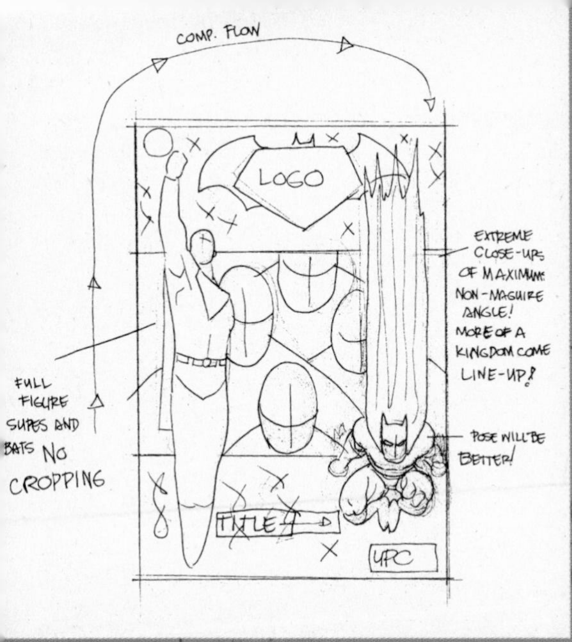
COMP. FLOW
LOGO
EXTREME CLOSE-UPS OF MAXIMUM NON-MAGUIRE ANGLE! MORE OF A KINGDOM COME LINE-UP!
FULL FIGURE SUPES AND BATS NO CROPPING
POSE WILL BE BETTER!
TITLE
UPC

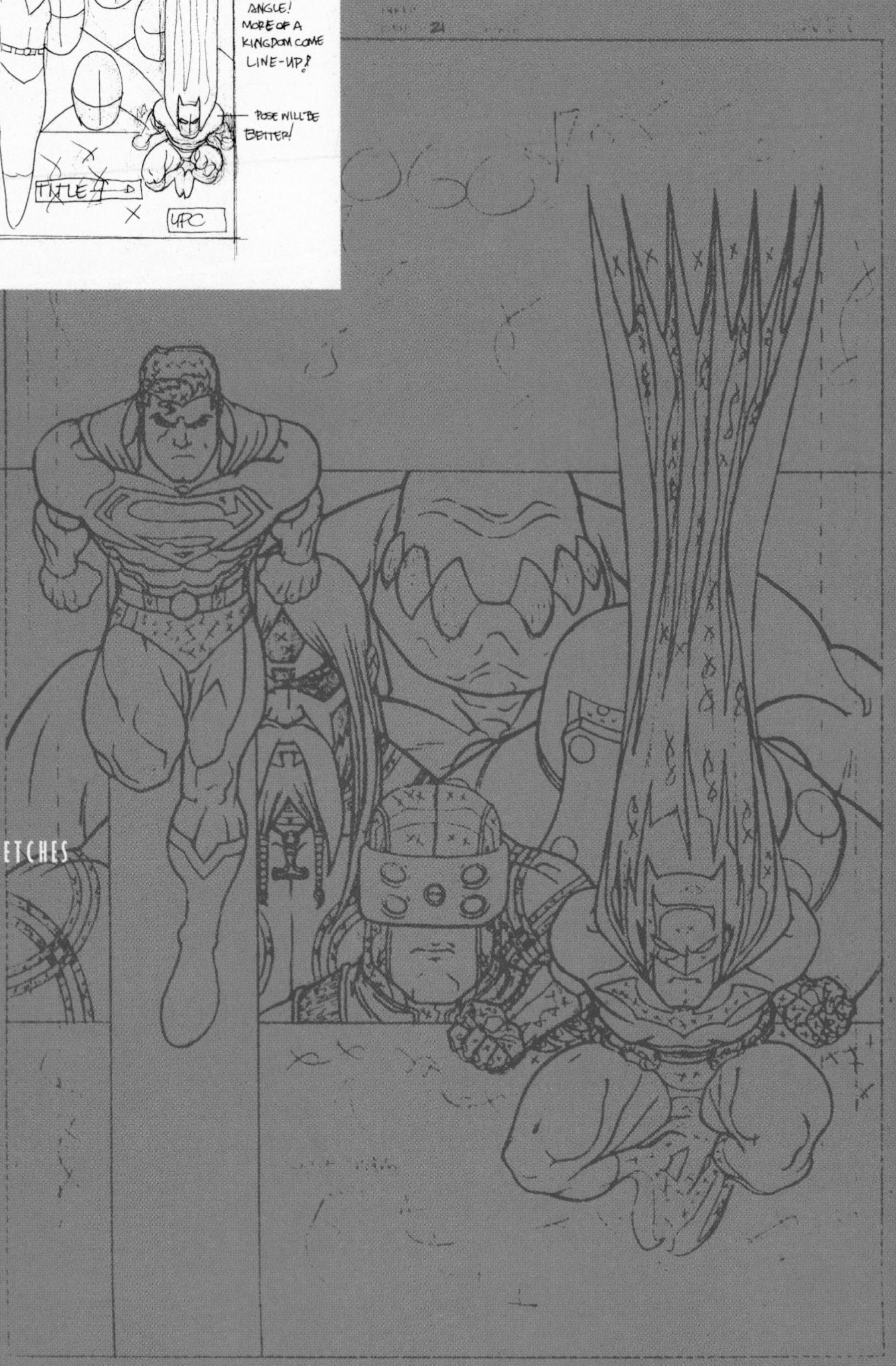

SKETCHES

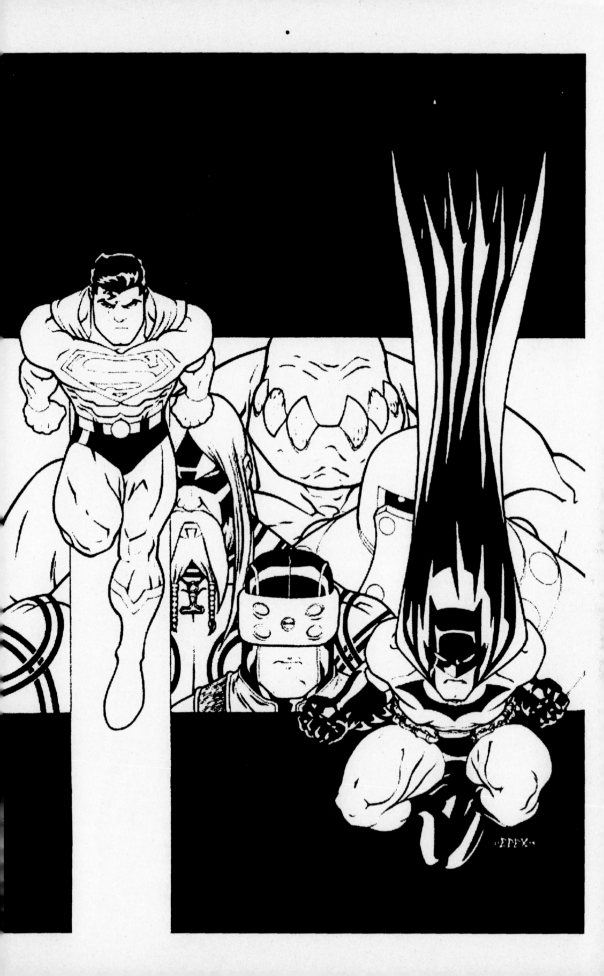

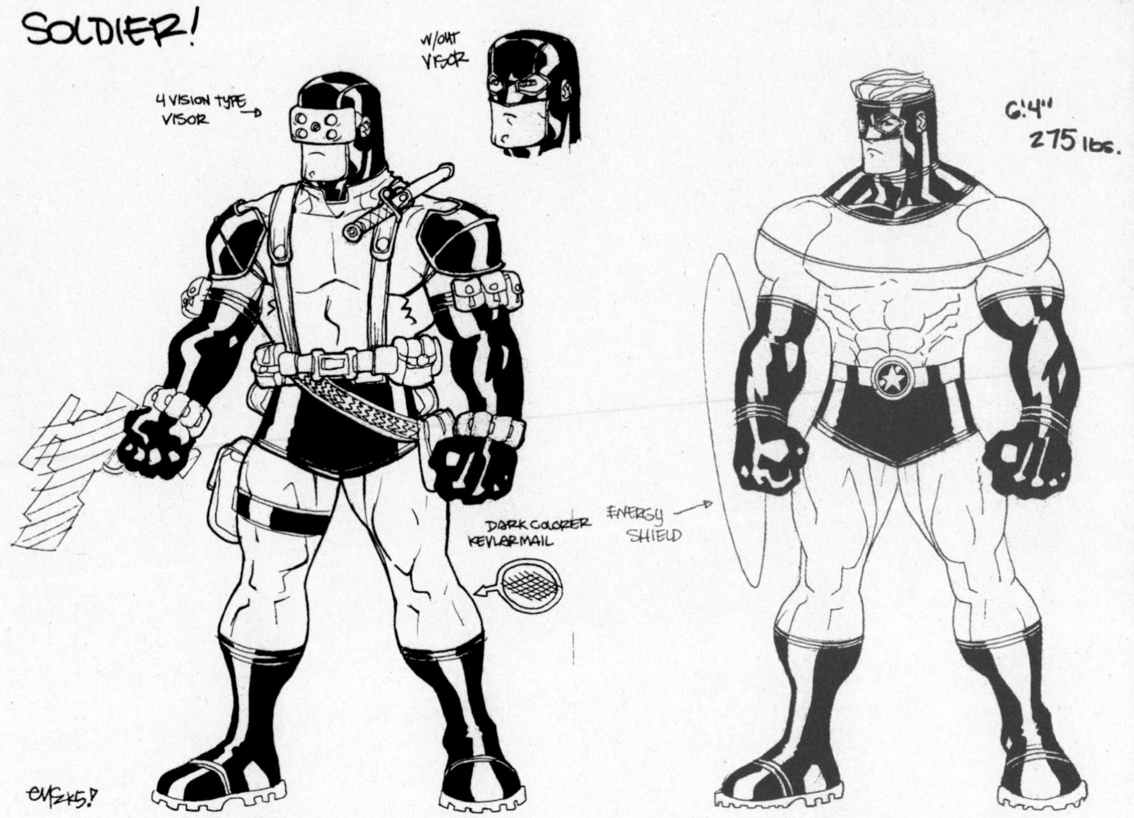
SOLDIER!
W/OUT VISOR
4 VISION TYPE VISOR
6'4"
275 lbs.
DARK COLORER KEVLARMAIL
ENERGY SHIELD

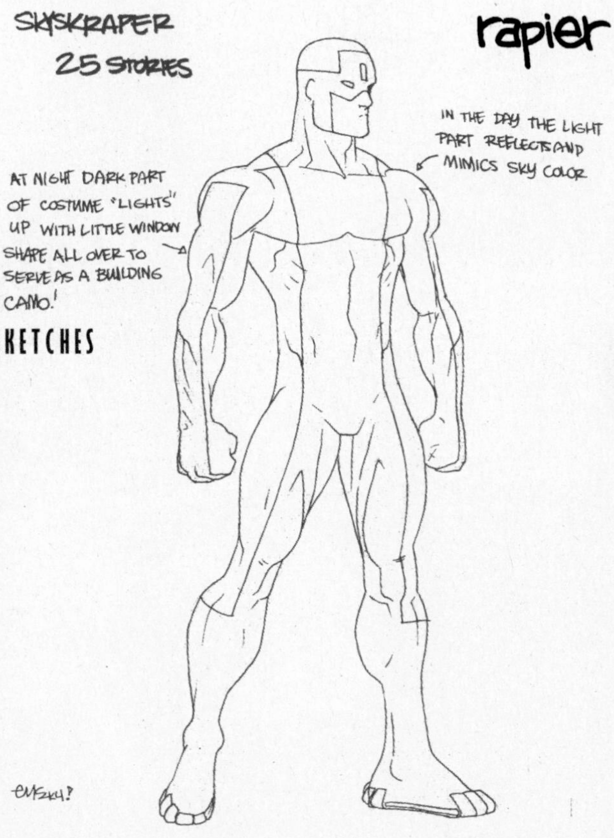
SKYSKRAPER
25 STORIES
IN THE DAY THE LIGHT PART REFLECTS AND MIMICS SKY COLOR
AT NIGHT DARK PART OF COSTUME "LIGHTS" UP WITH LITTLE WINDOW SHAPE ALL OVER TO SERVE AS A BUILDING CAMO!

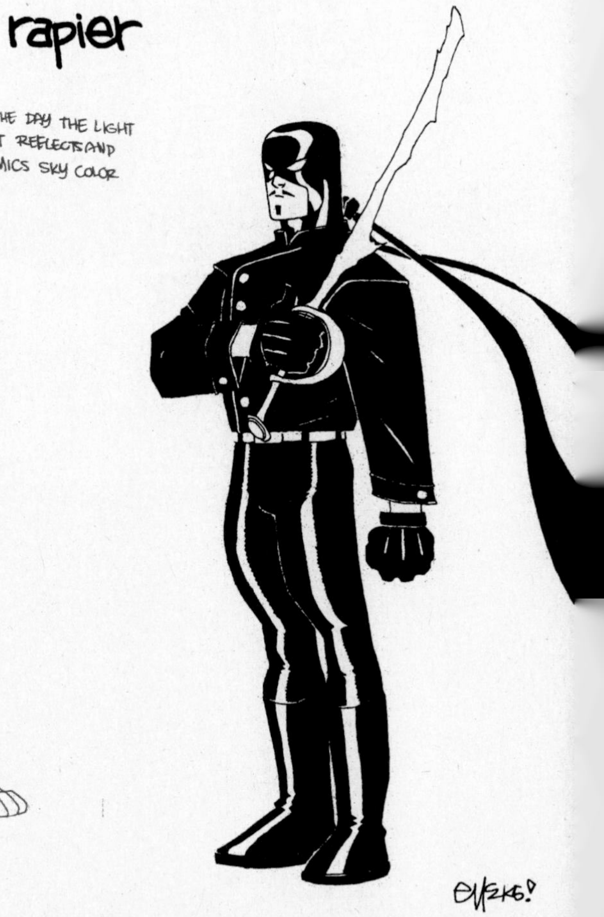
rapier

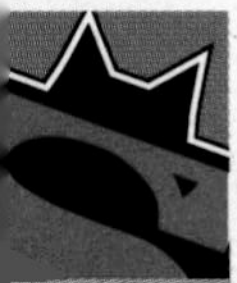

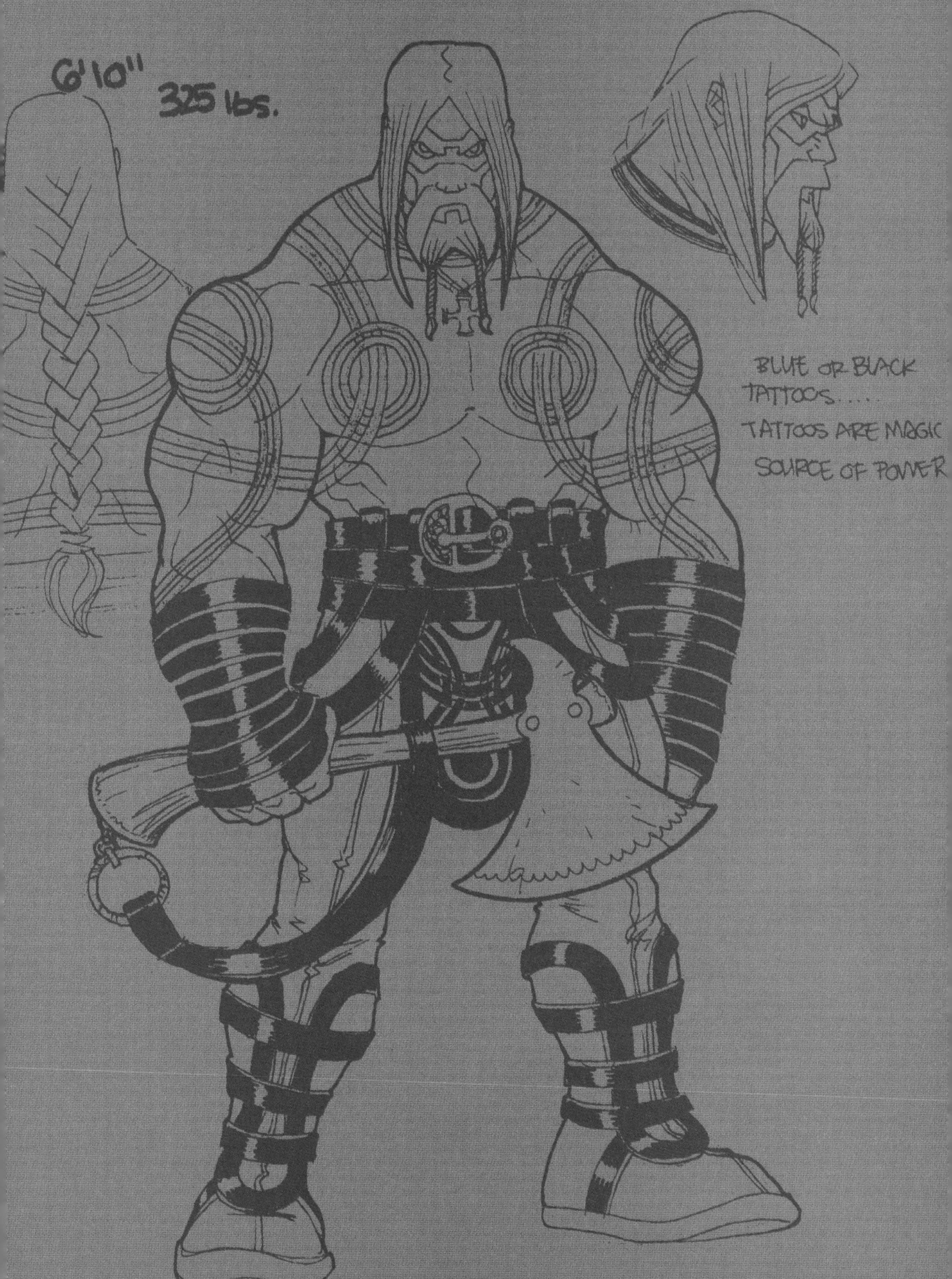
6'10"
325 lbs.
BLUE OR BLACK TATTOOS....
TATTOOS ARE MAGIC SOURCE OF POWER

BIOGRAPHIES

JEPH LOEB is the author of BATMAN: THE LONG HALLOWEEN, BATMAN: DARK VICTORY, SUPERMAN FOR ALL SEASONS, *Spider-Man: Blue, Daredevil: Yellow* and *Hulk: Gray*. A writer/producer living in Los Angeles, his credits include *Teen Wolf, Commando, Smallville* and *Lost*.

ED McGUINNESS first gained the notice of comic book fans with his work on *Deadpool* and *Vampirella*. His short run on WildStorm's MR. MAJESTIC landed him a gig on the monthly SUPERMAN title with Jeph Loeb, which led to the THUNDERCATS: RECLAIMING THUNDERA miniseries and arcs on SUPERMAN/BATMAN. He lives in Maine with his wife and four kids.

DEXTER VINES has been an inker in the comics industry for nearly a decade, having worked on numerous titles for various publishers, including *Uncanny X-Men, Weapon X* and *Wolverine* for Marvel Comics, *Meridian* for CrossGen Entertainment, and BATMAN: TENSES for DC.

DAVE STEWART began his career as an intern at Dark Horse Comics and then quickly moved into coloring comics. His credits include *Fray,* HUMAN TARGET: DIRECTOR'S CUT, SUPERMAN/BATMAN/ WONDER WOMAN: TRINITY, H-E-R-O and *Hellboy: The Third Wish* (for which he won an Eisner and Harvey Award). He lives in Portland, Oregon.

RICHARD STARKINGS is best known as the creator of the Comicraft studio, purveyors of unique design and fine lettering — and a copious catalogue of comic book fonts — since 1992. He is less well known as the creator and publisher of *Hip Flask* and his semi-autobiographical cartoon strip, *Hedge Backwards*. He never seems to get tired of reminding people that he lettered BATMAN: THE KILLING JOKE with a pen.

READ MORE OF THE MAN OF STEEL'S ADVENTURES IN THESE COLLECTIONS FROM DC COMICS:

SUPERMAN

SUPERMAN: FOR TOMORROW VOLUME 1

Brian Azzarello, Jim Lee and **Scott Williams** tell the epic tale of a cataclysmic event that strikes the Earth, affecting millions – including those closest to the Man of Steel.

BRIAN AZZARELLO JIM LEE SCOTT WILLIAMS
SUPERMAN
FOR TOMORROW
VOLUME ONE

"A BIG HERO NEEDS A BIG STORY, AND THIS TEAM DOESN'T DISAPPOINT."
— THE WASHINGTON POST

SUPERMAN: THE MAN OF STEEL VOLUME 1

JOHN BYRNE DICK GIORDANO
SUPERMAN
THE MAN OF STEEL

JOHN BYRNE
DICK GIORDANO

SUPERMAN FOR ALL SEASONS

Superman
For All Seasons
Jeph Loeb
Tim Sale
with Bjarne Hansen

JEPH LOEB
TIM SALE

THE DEATH OF SUPERMAN

THE BEST-SELLING GRAPHIC NOVEL OF ALL TIME!
THE DEATH OF
SUPERMAN
Dan Jurgens
Jerry Ordway
Louise Simonson
Roger Stern
Jon Bogdanove
Tom Grummett
Jackson Guice
Brett Breeding
Rick Burchett
Doug Hazlewood
Dennis Janke
Denis Rodier

DAN JURGENS
JERRY ORDWAY
JACKSON GUICE

SEARCH THE GRAPHIC NOVELS SECTION OF

www.DCCOMICS.com

FOR ART AND INFORMATION ON ALL OF OUR BOOKS!

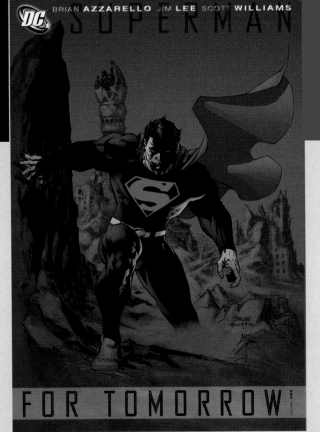

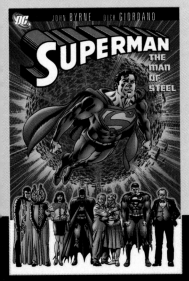

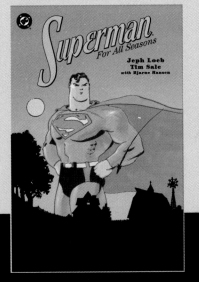